Reality Therapy
and
Choice Theory

Managing Behavior Today,
Developing Skills for Tomorrow

By Larry Myers
and David Jackson

American Correctional Association
Lanham, Maryland

a publication of the
AMERICAN CORRECTIONAL ASSOCIATION
Professional Development Department
4380 Forbes Boulevard
Lanham, MD 20706
1-800-222-5646
http://www.aca.org

MISSION STATEMENT

The American Correctional Association provides a professional organization for all individuals and groups, both public and private, that share a common goal of improving the justice system.

ISBN 1-56991-162-2

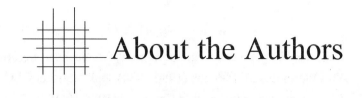# About the Authors

The authors have a rich background in working with juveniles—prevention programs, in mental health, on probation, in corrections and treatment programs—and in developing programs to work successfully with youth.

In 1955, Mr. David A Jackson, M.A., RTC, and Mr. Lawrence G. Myers, M.A., CCA began working with emotionally disturbed children together as childcare workers at Children Services of the Menninger Foundation in Topeka, Kansas.

In 1959, Mr. Jackson became a Juvenile Probation Officer with the Tulsa County Juvenile Court in Tulsa, Oklahoma. He moved up, in 1962, to the position of Director of Court Services and Interim Juvenile Judge. The Tulsa County Juvenile Court, in addition to full probation services, also operated The Lakeside Home, a co-educational treatment facility for delinquent juveniles. Mr. Jackson began seeing juveniles in groups while he was a probation officer. After he became Director, he continued doing group work with juveniles on probation and at The Lakeside Home.

Mr. Myers joined the staff as a Juvenile Probation Officer in 1962. As a Juvenile Probation Officer, Mr. Myers began doing group work with juveniles—not only at the Juvenile Court but also in a number of schools and institutions within the Tulsa area.

Mr. Jackson left the Juvenile Court in 1966 and became Executive Director of the Tulsa Mental Health Association, a position he held for the next three years. Afterward, he became the Assistant Chief Juvenile Probation officer in Tarrant County, Fort Worth, Texas, a position he held for the next 10 years. During this period, Mr. Jackson also was an Adjunct Professor at Texas Christian University in Fort Worth, Texas.

Following his tenure at Tarrant County, Mr. Jackson became Director of the Fort Worth Boys/Girls Club (1980-1984), and Publisher/CEO and Owner of TV Guide Advertising/Marketing Company (1984-1989).

During this time, Mr. Myers remained at the Tulsa County Juvenile Court as a Probation Officer (1962-1965), Probation Supervisor (1965-1971), Assistant Director (1971-1976) and then Director (1976-1979). In 1968, Tulsa County added a juvenile detention home to the Juvenile Bureau's operation.

For the years 1979-1984, Mr. Myers was Consultant/Partner of Team Associates, Inc., a management-consulting firm working with organizations to improve productivity and profit through the development of human resources.

In 1984, Mr. Myers became the Director of the Jackson County Juvenile Court, Kansas City, Missouri. Mr. Jackson joined him as Assistant Administrator in 1989. The Jackson County Juvenile Court operated two family attention centers, three group homes, a halfway house, a juvenile detention facility, a co-educational treatment facility for status offenders, a maximum-security facility for delinquent males, and, in conjunction with the Kansas City School System, an alternative school. Under their administration, the Court received five national awards.

Mr. Jackson became the Senior Instructor and Mid-American Regional Director for the William Glasser Institute in 1993, a position he holds at this time. Mr. Jackson, when he is not teaching and/or implementing Choice Theory and Reality Therapy within juvenile correctional facilities, can be reached at:

Heartland Center for Personal & Professional Development
20837 Coon Branch Road
Lawson, Missouri 64062
Phone: 816/580-4275; Fax: 816/580-3011
Email: cty32420@centurytel.com

Mr. Myers left the Jackson County Juvenile Court in 1994 and spent two and one half years as Juvenile Projects Director for the American Correctional Association. Since 1996, he has been the Municipal Court Administrator in Joplin, Missouri. Mr. Myers can be reached at:

Joplin Municipal Court
303 East Third Street
Joplin, Missouri 64801
Phone: 417/624-0820 Ext. 236; Fax: 417/625-7534
Email: LMyers@joplinmo.org

Mr. Jackson and Mr. Myers have joined forces, once again, in writing *Reality Therapy and Choice Theory: Managing Behavior Today, Developing Skills for Tomorrow*. They believe you will find the information and techniques helpful not only in your work with juveniles but also in your personal life.

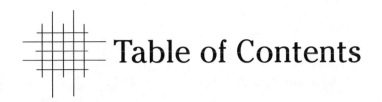

Table of Contents

A note from the authors:

"This workbook is for ANYONE working with youth. Counseling includes the interaction not only of the assigned therapist but also those coming into daily contact with the youth—careworkers, teachers, cooks, bus drivers, custodians and so forth. The RELATIONSHIPS developed with the child, regardless of who the adult is, are the MOST IMPORTANT part of ANY treatment program. We have addressed this issue in the scenarios provided in the workbook. If you are a careworker (line officer), you are constantly modeling and encouraging youth to LEARN better ways of living their lives. In this respect, you are counseling. Remember that ALL counseling is teaching."

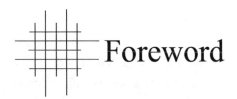

Foreword

As the authors of *Reality Therapy and Choice Theory: Managing Behavior Today, Developing Skills for Tomorrow* point out, those of us working in the juvenile justice field "see juveniles who engage in self-destructive behaviors. We see juveniles who do not have good parent-child and/or teacher-student relationships. We see juveniles who have acquaintances but not friends. To help juveniles make better choices, we need to help them improve their relationships with others—and that begins with us."

Research has shown that punishment is not effective either as a deterrent or in reducing recidivism in the long run. Punishment relies on *external* control. In contrast, cognitive-behavioral programs are among the most effective interventions. They rely upon *internal* control. One of the building blocks of Choice Theory is that we can control only our own behavior. Therefore, we are responsible for making the correct choices to control our behavior.

Implementing Reality Therapy and Choice Theory in a juvenile facility helps juveniles learn to make the right choices, to rely upon internal control. Staff learn to use the concepts, both at work and at home, and teach them to juveniles. In learning to use the concepts, staff learn how to give up common ways of attempts to control behavior: criticizing, blaming, complaining, threatening, punishing, nagging and rewarding. The result is less conflict, improved relationships, and a better outlook on life.

The theory behind Reality Therapy is Choice Theory. Reality Therapy is how we build a working relationship with those we are helping. *Reality Therapy and Choice Theory: Managing Behavior Today, Developing Skills for Tomorrow* teaches us how to implement Reality Therapy and Choice Theory in a juvenile facility. The authors rely upon their extensive experience of teaching and using the concepts with both staff and juveniles throughout the United States. The authors provide examples of working with different types of youths in a variety of settings. The questions at the end of the chapters give readers an opportunity to check their understanding before moving on to the next chapter.

We hope that this workbook helps you learn how to make positive changes in your life and to teach juveniles how to do the same.

Yours truly,

James A. Gondles, Jr. C.A.E.
Executive Director
American Correctional Association

 # Introduction

By William Glasser, M.D.

Starting in 1956, the first 11 years of my career were spent working as the staff psychiatrist at the Ventura School for Girls, a California Youth Authority Institution in Camarillo, California. In the new institution, we had 400 girls, ages 15 to 19. During this time, I learned a lot and contributed a great deal to the development of the program. I was a long way from creating the Choice Theory described in this book. But I can see, in retrospect, that Choice Theory was the basic psychology that we used at Ventura.

We were very successful because we did not punish and because we ran a school in which almost all the girls succeeded. What we did is explained clearly in this workbook. Many correctional institutions fail to succeed. They spend more time in holding people than in teaching them how to live their lives so that they do not get into trouble. The only way that can be done is to get a substantial amount of external control out of the program and replace it with Choice Theory. At Ventura, we got rid of almost all of it.

Choice Theory is clear and easy to learn, but it is hard to do, especially in corrections because the tradition there is all external control. What David and Larry have written is a specific "how to" workbook that explains what to do clearly in your correctional situation. Getting started is difficult because Choice Theory is such a different way to treat offenders. But if you do, they will get a lot of help.

The best thing and the easiest thing to do is to teach it directly to the offenders. As they learn it, talk to them about what they used to do that they don't do now. If they can begin to put Choice Theory to work in their lives—both in and out of an institution—they will begin to take responsibility for their behavior, something few do now. If you are patient and persist, you will have a lot of success. But resist trying to make them learn it. That will defeat your efforts.

William Glasser, M.D., President of the William Glasser Institute

13

CHAPTER 1

 History and Overview

Objectives

After reading this chapter, you will be able to:

- Identify at least four books written by William Glasser
- List three levels of external control
- Identify the one thing Glasser believes to be the problem of the world
- Explain why Choice Theory replaced Control Theory
- Describe how Choice Theory can help you improve your personal relationships at home, in the community, and at work

In this chapter, you will learn some of the history of Choice Theory and Reality Therapy and how they developed. Choice Theory believes that the major problem of the world is external control psychology. We believe that we can control other people and make them do things, even if they don't want to do them. External control psychology creates destruction and problems in our personal and professional relationships. The concepts of Choice Theory and Reality Therapy will not only change your outlook on life but also improve all of your relationships—at home, in the community, and at work (if used properly).

Introductory History

The authors first heard of Reality Therapy in 1967 while working in the juvenile court in Tulsa, Oklahoma. A junior league case aide brought in an article from the June issue of Harper's magazine written by Jack Langguth entitled, *"California's Gift to Psychotherapy."* Several quotes in the article caught the attention of the authors. Among them were:

- "One psychiatric guidebook already lists thirty-six forms of treatment, from Assertion-Structured Therapy to Will Therapy. That's without Dr. Glasser. Why Number 37? Because Reality Therapy seems to work, and a lot of the others don't," Langguth says. He goes on to say that he does not want Reality Therapy "to settle into a respectable niche in the textbooks but to be widely practiced—among other places—in prisons, mental hospitals, and slum schools."

- "Three out of four girls get out of Ventura and then stay out—which is no better than the success rate of several other California institutions. **But there is a measurable difference**. While they are at Ventura, these angry, scarred girls show less disruptive behavior than before they were incarcerated. For the first time in their lives, the girls experienced success in school. And when they leave, their lives run smoother and straighter than their predecessors. They are more responsible than when they entered Ventura."

- ". . . the psychiatrist cannot sit by silently while you hash over the failures of your past. He must give of himself, his ideas, and his thinking. A patient often has no one to care about him. The therapist must care. He must become involved. Even better, he should get the members of various groups involved with each other."

- "We're not looking for whose fault it is. We're looking for how we can fix it."

- "Whether you are dealing with truants or mainliners, the vital thing is to be personal. Tell the addict or the delinquent in every way you can, 'It's important to me what happens to you. I care about you.'"
- "Every child starts out in life with confidence in his own worth and with trust in the world around him."
- We were looking for "what worked." Many of our fellow juvenile probation officers believed that the way to work with juvenile offenders was to: tell them what you expect, set the probation rules, and then check on them. If you catch them in a violation, their probation is revoked. However, we were stressing involvement with the youth and families that we were working with on probation. The concepts in the article hit home and fit with what we were trying to accomplish.

Prior to Langguth's article, Glasser had written *Mental Health or Mental Illness?: Psychiatry for Practical Action* in 1961, and *Reality Therapy: A New Approach to Psychiatry* in 1965. We read *Reality Therapy*, and we found the concepts to be easily understood and easily applied. We began to dabble with the concepts. We attended workshops on Reality Therapy and began to use it more extensively.

Early on, we saw the influence that Reality Therapy was having on the field of juvenile and adult corrections. Glasser attended Case Institute of Technology, and by age 19, he was a chemical engineer. Perhaps this background led to the logical steps that correctional practitioners found appealing with Reality Therapy. They liked the six ways that Reality Therapy differed from conventional psychotherapy. They liked the 13 steps for involvement. They liked the concept of holding offenders responsible for and accountable for their behavior. They liked discussing the "here and now" and found it to be more useful than discussing "the past" in working with offenders. They liked having a clear "cookbook approach" on how to work with offenders. They liked the way Reality Therapy took the "treatment" out of a closed-door office and put it on the floor of the unit—where everyone could see it and be a part of it.

After Glasser wrote *Schools without Failure* in 1969, we brought him to Tulsa. More than 500 probation officers, schoolteachers, therapists, practitioners and college students in the community attended his workshop.

We watched with interest as the theory developed with the books that followed: *Positive Addiction* and *The Identity Society*, both published in 1972; *Control Theory*, published in 1984; and *Control Theory in the Practice of Reality Therapy: Case Studies*, published in 1989.

We also watched the misuse of Reality Therapy and Control Theory as practitioners tried to use it without establishing personal involvement with the people supposedly being helped. "Reality" and "responsibility" often were used as verbal clubs with which to beat offenders about their heads and shoulders for their transgressions. Reality Therapy is a therapy, which focuses on the present problem to get the offender's attention. Without the personal involvement with the therapist, there will be no connecting, and the therapy will not hold the offender's attention.

Building relationships was (and often continues to be) foreign to correctional officers. In fact, many of the helping professions cautioned about getting overly emotionally involved with the client. Some juvenile justice staff interpreted this warning to mean "no involvement" with the juveniles. We believe, as Glasser does, that all people fulfill their basic needs by being involved with other people. Without our involvement, Reality Therapy simply becomes another way to control and manipulate the juveniles with whom we are working.

Building a relationship with juvenile offenders is a concept often resisted by juvenile careworkers. The mere thought, if not taboo, is repugnant to many careworkers and their supervisors. The concept of building relationships and maintaining personal involvement is one area where we continue to find a lot of resistance. Yet, it is the most potent tool that we have in working with juveniles. We will discuss this issue throughout the workbook because Choice

Theory believes that the major human problems we struggle with are caused by unsatisfying relationships.

Glasser saw that the words "Control Theory" were adding to the misuse and misunderstanding of both the theory behind Reality Therapy and Reality Therapy itself. He realized that the control needs to be internal and not external. External control harms everyone, both the controllers and the controlled.

Dr. Glasser was speaking in Sydney, Australia during an extended lecture tour in 1996. He found himself saying the same things he was saying in 1986, 1976, 1966, and probably in 1956. They were good things on how to help people with emotional problems, but the problems still existed. Something must be wrong! Reality Therapy was not the only method of helping people. Universities with counseling and psychology departments, social workers, and psychiatric professionals were all saying things to help people. But no one was addressing the underlying problem that continued to create the symptomatic problems.

At this point, Dr. Glasser realized what the problem of the world was and is—external control psychology!

He later wrote: "I had not spent enough time examining and explaining external control psychology. It is the menace of our society, and it is the way we have lived our lives since birth. Our grandparents lived by external control. Their grandparents, and so on, and so on. Our parents taught us directly about external control. Our teachers reinforced the concept that 'I can make you do anything I want you to, even if you don't want to do it,' and our bosses used it on us, and we have taught our own children this dreaded way of dealing with each other."

Glasser says that there are three levels of external control. First, an external stimulus supposedly makes us do something. If the telephone rings, we think we answer it because of the ring. If the light turns red, we stop because the light turned red.

David says: "If the latter were true, I would have died at the first red light in Tyler, Texas on the night of April 4, 1985 just three minutes after midnight. I had gone to Lake Palestine to fish awhile before the sun fell on that lovely spring afternoon. There was no one else at my favorite spot just below the dam on a beautiful little stream. I fished for a while and had caught two nice catfish and missed one big one. Though darkness approached, I continued to fish as a big, gorgeous harvest moon rose over the creek. I was enjoying my freedom through the solitude of being with nature, and I chose to neglect the time. It was 11:30 p.m. when I finally gathered up my gear and walked through tall grass to the car. As I reached for the door of my car, I was struck on the left ankle by a copperhead snake. I quickly got into my car and drove to Tyler. There were six stoplights between the city limits and the emergency room at the hospital. All six lights turned red as I approached them. If the stimulus of the red light had 'made' me react by stopping, I would still be at the first red light. I chose to run each and every one of them and reached the hospital where I was successfully treated."

Glasser explains that neither the ring of the phone nor the red of the light "makes" us do anything. The ring and the red are important to us because they are information. We take in the information through our sensory system, recognize it, and put value on it as to how we will choose to behave with this new information. This first step of external control psychology is not destructive, but the second and third levels are destructive to relationships.

The second level is that I can make you do something I want you to do even if you don't want to do it. Or, you can make me do something you want me to do whether I want to or not. We see this belief acted out in families, classrooms, businesses, probation offices, and correctional facilities. The belief hasn't worked for over 100 years. Yet, we continue to do it and even increase the external control when it doesn't seem to be working. Why pour gasoline on a fire you are trying to put out?

The third level of external control is the most destructive of all. I will make you do it because it is right, even if I have to kill you to do it. We witnessed the most extreme of this level on September 11, 2001 when nearly 3,000 people perished in two world trade centers in New York City. Over 150 individuals died in the attack on the Pentagon building, headquarters of the U.S. Department of Defense. The terrorists will make the rest of the world do what they want because it is "the right thing to do." That kind of righteousness is the most destructive of all the external control behaviors.

Glasser believes that the external control the majority of the world lives by is the basis of all human miseries, aside from extreme poverty and untreatable physical illness. Only until the world can accept and practice Choice Theory will there be some resolution of the human problems that we continually keep treating. The DSMIV is full of the symptoms of externally motivated psychology. Choice Theory says that all behavior is intrinsic or internal and that we choose all of our purposeful behaviors.

Glasser's beliefs about external control theory led to his book *Choice Theory: A New Psychology of Personal Freedom*, published in 1998. Choice Theory is an internal control psychology; it explains why and how we make the choices in our lives. Choice Theory replaced Control Theory. Choice Theory teaches us that we are much more in control of our own lives than we are aware.

In 2000, Glasser wrote *Reality Therapy in Action*, which is also published in paperback as *Counseling with Choice Theory: The New Reality Therapy*. In this book, Glasser invites you into his office to sit with him and his clients as he practices Reality Therapy using Choice Theory.

In 2002, Glasser wrote *Unhappy Teenagers: A Way for Parents and Teachers to Reach Them*. In this book, Glasser explains a way for parents and teachers to teach youth. He continues to spotlight the importance of connecting relationships.

We will present the concepts of both Choice Theory and Reality Therapy in this workbook. To fully understand Choice Theory and Reality Therapy, you must understand the concepts of basic needs, quality worlds, total behavior, and creative systems. Although we will discuss each concept in the following chapters, we will define them briefly to give you an overall understanding and a foundation for learning.

Choice Theory and Reality Therapy are a systems approach. They contain key parts that work together.

Choice Theory provides the theoretical basis for the practice of Reality Therapy. It consists of basic needs, quality worlds, total behavior, and creative systems, which provide the basis for a new psychology of personal freedom.

Reality Therapy is a method of helping people—in our case, juveniles—take better control of their lives. RT helps people identify what they want and what they need. RT then helps them evaluate whether they can realistically attain what they want without interfering with others' ability to satisfy their needs.

The key parts of the system are:

- **Basic needs**—As humans, we have genetic needs that are a blueprint for how we will attempt to live our lives.
- **Total behavior** consists of four components that are present in every behavior—acting, thinking, feeling and physiology.
- **Quality world**—A quality world is like a photo album where each of us puts those pictures (perceptions) that are most pleasing to us (most need satisfying). If we don't like a picture, we don't include it in our photo album (quality world).
- **Creative system**—A creative system is the spontaneous activity of new ideas, or the reorganizing of old ideas to create new ideas.

We invite you to sit with us as we work with a variety of youth in situations you may find within your facility. We will discuss concepts, tools and techniques that will be useful in your work with juvenile offenders.

This material will change your outlook on life and, if used and taught to others, will improve all of your relationships at home and at work. You will see less conflict in your institution. You will find the youth more pleasant to work with and easier to manage. You also will find youth experiencing more success in school, in the facility, and in their home, once they are released.

Summary

Choice Theory and Reality Therapy have evolved over the past 35 years and continue to evolve. According to Glasser, external control psychology is the major cause of problems in the world. The three levels of external control psychology are:

1. An external stimulus makes us do something. If the telephone rings, we think we answer it because of the ring. The ring does not make us do anything, however. It is information that we recognize, and we put value on it as to how we will choose to behave with this new information. This level of external control psychology is not destructive.
2. I can make you do something I want you to do even if you don't want to do it. Or, you can make me do something you want me to do whether I want to do it or not. This second level of external control psychology is destructive and has not worked, yet we continue to try and make it work.
3. I will make you do it because it is right, even if I have to kill you to do it. This third level of external control psychology is the most destructive of all levels of external control behaviors.

The only person we have control over is ourselves, and we are much more in control of our own lives than we are aware. Once we realize how much internal control we have, we can begin practicing Choice Theory and teach it to others. As a result of these efforts, our personal and professional lives will improve. At work, we will find less conflict and will find the youth more manageable and the environment more enjoyable. Youth will seek us out for advice and problem solving; they will experience more success in and outside of the facility.

Questions

1. List four books written by Dr. William Glasser.

   a._____

   b._____

   c._____

   d._____

2. Glasser's concern that the words _____ _____ were adding to the misuse and misunderstanding of Reality Therapy lead to _____ _____.

3. Both Control Theory and Choice Theory are examples of _____ control psychology.

4. True/False. Choice Theory is of value only in working with juveniles at work.

5. According to Glasser, what is the problem of the world?

   _____

6. List three levels of external control:

- _____

- _____

- _____

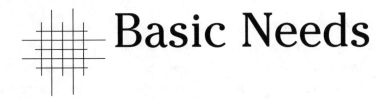

CHAPTER 2

Basic Needs

Objectives

After reading this chapter, you will be able to:

- List the five basic needs we all have:
    1) the four psychological needs, and
    2) the one psychological need
- Identify the need unique to our species

Introduction

Everyone has needs. Choice Theory believes that our five basic needs are to:

- Survive and reproduce
- Belong and be loved
- Have power
- Have freedom
- Have fun

Needs, especially the needs for power and freedom, are hard for juveniles in custody to meet in a responsible manner. In this chapter, we will discuss basic needs and give some examples of how needs of juveniles in your facility can be met.

Basic Needs

Dr. William Glasser believes our five basic needs are genetic in nature and are a blueprint for how we try to live our lives. According to Glasser, needs are like a motor in a car that provide the power which drives us. He says, "All our behavior is always our best choice to satisfy one or more of these needs."

Glasser talks about five basic needs: the one physiological need, found in the old brain, is the need to survive and reproduce. The four psychological needs, found in the new brain (the cerebral cortex), are the need to belong and be loved, the need for power, the need for freedom, and the need for fun.

The brain is the organ that controls how an individual views the world. Information is processed and choices on how to satisfy one or more of basic needs are made based upon the information. The brain is complex, but it can be viewed as two interconnected, self-regulating parts—the "old and new brains." All higher animals, even fish, have an "old brain" that is located at the center of the brain. The "old brain" is where the physiological need to survive is found. It controls the basic functions of life, such as breathing, hunger, and sexual drive. If the old brain stops operating, the body dies.

The "new brain," or cortex, surrounds the old brain. The four psychological needs are located in the cortex.

Let's look now at the five basic needs.

The One Physiological Need
The Need to Survive and Reproduce

We need to breathe to stay alive. If we become short of breath, we become preoccupied with breathing. Everyone else becomes unimportant. Fortunately, we do not have to think about breathing. Our brain takes care of that for us—even if we try not to breathe by holding our breath.

We all have heard about people who have lived for years while in a deep coma. These individuals are incapable of any conscious decision to breathe or perform any other bodily functions that would be life sustaining. Their brain automatically (autonomic system) tells their bodies what to do to sustain life.

We don't mean to imply that people can't decide to try to take their own lives or even try to place themselves in harms way. If people are having emotional problems or facing a terminal physical illness, they may decide they want to die. Each of us knows juveniles who, through their own behavior, are placing themselves at risk and may even have a fatalistic attitude toward death.

Within each of us there is the genetic need to survive. When we can't get air, food, or water, our mind automatically tells our body what to do to stay alive or, at least, to prolong life. We sweat when we are hot, and we shiver when we are cold. We do this even if we decide to try to interfere with these basic functions. For example, a 5-year-old may threaten to hold his breath. Even if he holds it until he passes out, which is unlikely, the old brain automatically will tell the body to start breathing again.

While sex is not necessary for our own survival, the need to reproduce is important to perpetuate the species. As we move toward adulthood, our urge for sexual release becomes stronger.

Our need to survive and to reproduce is strong. However, people can starve themselves, as do anorexics and hunger strikers, or renounce sex, as do priests and nuns. These are conscious decisions to override the survival and reproduction need because of other values considered more important than staying alive or reproducing.

The Four Psychological Needs
The Need to Belong and to Be Loved

We all have a need to belong. Ways to satisfy this need include belonging to a family, having friends, and being part of a team, club, gang, or an organization.

Author Henry David Thoreau knew the strength of this need when he wrote, "No man is an island unto himself." We have a need to belong. People may choose to be alone, but nobody chooses to be lonely.

Being a part of a family is where we get and give love, where we love and are loved in return. We also satisfy this need outside the family in social situations and at work. Through these activities of loving, sharing and cooperating, we can develop meaningful and, hopefully, healthy relationships that satisfy our basic need. We also develop relationships that lead us to marry and to develop families of our own.

The need to belong is so basic and so strong that it can override the need to survive. For example, most people who commit or attempt suicide say that loneliness was the cause. The need for love and belonging is the most difficult of the four psychological needs to satisfy because we cannot satisfy this need by ourselves.

The Need for Power

Power appears to be unique to our species. Choice Theory views power as competence, achievement, self-worth, status, recognition, importance, and competition. We have a need to be seen as competent, and we have a need to achieve. We have a need for status, importance, and recognition. We all like to be recognized for doing a good job. At a minimum, we want someone to listen to what we have to say. In Choice Theory, all of these are grouped together under the need for power.

According to Glasser, " . . . at a minimum, we want someone to listen to what we have to say. If no one listens to us, we feel the pain of the powerless, the kind of pain you feel in a foreign country when you are trying to get information, and no one speaks your language." (Glasser, *Choice Theory*)

Our need for power may cause direct conflict with our need to belong. Glasser says, "People marry for love and belonging; but once married, driven by the need for power, they struggle to take control of the relationship." (Glasser, *Choice Theory*) A person may sacrifice the marriage for power. Similarly, an individual may sacrifice a relationship with a child for power.

Glasser also believes that we differ from all other living creatures in our need for power. Wanting power "for the sake of power" is unique to human beings. We are the only "power driven species."

Power is detrimental to relationships when it is used to dominate another or others. In his book *Unhappy Teenagers, A Way for Parents and Teachers to Reach Them*, Glasser says, "The only way we can satisfy our needs for both love and power is to gain the respect, trust, and love of the people in our lives. If we try to control them, we may maintain their love, but we will never gain their respect or trust. When we are respected, trusted and loved, we feel powerful; we neither need nor want anyone to fear us." (Glasser, *Unhappy Teenagers*)

The Need for Freedom

The need for freedom is the need for independence, for autonomy, to move around freely, and for the freedom to make choices. The United States is based on our need for freedom. People from Europe came to this country for freedom; freedom to worship as they wished; freedom of speech; freedom to read what they wanted to read; freedom to write what they wanted to write; freedom to associate with whom they wanted to associate—in short, freedom to pursue happiness as they chose.

Freedom is so basic a need that people will give up their life fighting for it.

Glasser believes that the need for freedom is an attempt to "provide the correct balance between your need to try to force me to live my life the way you want and my need to be free of that force. This balance is best expressed by the golden rule: Do unto others as you would have others do unto you." (Glasser, *Choice Theory*) Creativity is stifled when freedom is stifled.

The Need for Fun

Someone once said that play is how we learn to cope with the world. Glasser believes that if we are not having fun, no learning is taking place. Learning must be fun. Fun is the genetic reward for learning. Think back and remember the teachers who taught you a lot. Did you have fun in their class? Chances are that they taught classes in such a way that you and others had fun.

There are so many ways to have fun and rarely do others stand in our way to have fun. They like to have fun too and will join in with us.

Glasser points out that most of us do not feel as driven by fun as we are by power, freedom, or belonging. However, he believes that fun is as much a basic need as any other. When individuals leave a relationship because they want their freedom, they also might be leaving because they have ceased having fun and learning within that relationship. In marriages that go sour, fun usually is the first casualty.

According to Glasser, "… we are the only creatures who play all our lives. And because we do, we learn all our lives. The day we stop playing is the day we stop learning." (Glasser, *Choice Theory*)

Characteristics of Needs

Glasser believes that needs are our ultimate source of motivation. As we stated at the beginning of this section, our needs are like a motor in a car. They provide the power that drives our behavior to get us what we want.

Needs are general and are universal. They are general in that what satisfies a need for one person may not satisfy the same need for another person. Yet, they are universal in that we all have the same needs.

Needs may conflict with one another. Consequently, satisfying our needs may involve a process of give and take. For example, we may satisfy our need to belong by sacrificing our need for power, our need to be the decision-maker. Glasser discusses another example: "Freedom is the freedom from others but never all others…therefore, our need for freedom may be in conflict with our need to be loved and to belong, and we have to balance these needs to avoid conflict in our relationships."

Just as our needs may be in conflict with one another, satisfying our needs may be in conflict with others satisfying their needs. We must learn to satisfy our needs in a way that doesn't hinder others from satisfying their needs.

The last trait of needs is that they are fulfilled from moment to moment. They are never permanently satisfied. The need for belonging and love, power, freedom, and fun are like the need for food. After you eat, you are not hungry, but in time, you will be.

One of the hardest needs to meet in a facility in socially approved ways is the need for power. The following scenario may help you see how needs in general and the need for power specifically are met within your facility. The scenario is of Josh and Jay T.

Josh and Jay T.

I (David) was visiting a correctional facility and conducting training on Reality Therapy for some of the youth workers. One day after my class, one of the youth workers approached me. He asked if I would see a couple of students who were having trouble, to try to make a difference. He said that the staff had tried punishing, threatening, lecturing and using physical restraints to no avail. I agreed to see the boys.

In a group meeting conducted by one of the youth workers, 16-year-old Josh and 17-year-old Jay T. had a confrontation that erupted into a fistfight. This fight was not their first.

The consequence for this kind of infraction is either a minor OR (Observation Report) or a major OR, at the discretion of the worker involved. ORs are detrimental to the youths advancing from one level to another, with the fifth level the one to be reached prior to dismissal from the institution. Jay T. is at Level Five, and Josh is at Level Four. The youth worker began to give me the background of each youngster and what had happened in group.

In counseling with Choice Theory, the past has little use—unless there is something in the client's past that has been successful in a similar situation as the present problem. Otherwise, if we missed last week's dinner, it's gone. We can never eat that dinner, and if we had an unpleasant past, why live through that unpleasantness a second time. We can make choices only for the here and now.

In this case, what happened in the group session is relevant. The youth worker told me that the two boys had argued and then each had hit the other one. The worker said that he had written a major OR. He was holding it until he found out if I would see the boys and make them stop fighting. I told him I couldn't make anybody do anything but would see if I could persuade them to try something different and better than fighting.

The boys were sitting apart on hard benches just outside the office where we would talk.

Worker: "Boys, this is Mr. Jackson, and he is going to talk with you about your fighting. Mr. Jackson, this is Josh and Jay T."

David: I nodded to both boys. "Hi guys, let's go into the office where we can find more comfortable chairs. O.K.?"

They both nodded, grunted something that sounded like "uh-huh," and followed me into the office. I moved the chairs so that I would be sitting between them with my chair back just a little—so that I could look at either of them as we talked.

After we were seated, I said: "Hey, guys. I'll make a deal with you. Are you interested?"

Josh:	He was a little suspicious. "What kind of deal?"
Jay T.:	But Jay said: "I'm ready for a deal if it will get me out of having an OR written up on me."
David:	"This is just a simple deal. I like to be called Dave. May I call you by your first names?"

They both looked at me as if I had stepped out of a spaceship.

Jay T.:	"Hey, that's cool man, uh Dave. The workers would never let us call them by their first names."
Josh:	"You got that right. Just who are you, and what do you do?"
David:	"I travel around the country working with counselors, teachers, careworkers and others who work with guys like you, and I try to help make things better. Now, what did you boys want to see me about?"

My job is to connect with these youngsters. So, I often do something unexpected rather than the external control psychology that they are expecting which will drive us farther apart. I must get closer to them to have a chance of helping them.

Jay T.:	"Hey! We are here because we were told to be here."
Josh:	"Yeah, what are you going to do to us?"
David:	"I'm not going to do anything to you. I just thought we could talk a little bit and see if we could become friends. Is that all right?"
Josh:	"Sure. Why would you want to make friends with us? It's really about our fighting isn't it?"
Jay T.:	"Are we getting majors?"
David:	"I'm not giving you anything but my friendship, and maybe help you with some ideas on what would make it better for you while you are in here. Would you like for it to be better?"

Jay T.:	"Yeah, but . . . can you come back each week?"
Josh:	"Yeah, if you can come back each week maybe that would make it better."
David:	"If you had a car and one of the tires went flat, wouldn't you like to know how to change it yourself, and make things better yourself? Then you wouldn't need someone else to change your tire, would you?"

Both boys thought about this for some time. That is good. I want them to spend time thinking and doing rather than spending a lot of time thinking or talking about feelings. The boys can arbitrarily change their thinking and acting but not their feelings. Otherwise, I could say, "cheer up guys," and my job would be over.

| Jay T.: | "But Josh is such a liar, and he is always lying about every thing and . . ." |
| David: | "Let me interrupt you a moment Jay T. If you can hold that thought we will get back to it. Josh, I will be asking you what you think is wrong with Jay T., but first can I just ask a few questions?" |

Anytime I can ask them for permission or their ideas, I am helping them satisfy their power needs. Youth in this setting have difficulty satisfying their power needs in a socially acceptable manner.

| Josh: | "Well, yeah, but you really need to know some things about Jay T. He is a real jerk." |
| David: | "OK, OK. We'll get to both your complaints in a moment, but first I really do need your permission to ask a few more questions. OK?" |

Both boys agreed that I could ask some questions.

Jay T.:	"I guess you want to know what we did to get sent here, huh?"
David:	"No, I'm really not interested in that. Whatever it was, it's done. We can't undo what's done. We can only start now to live our lives in a better way to get what we want—if what we want is not going to get us into more trouble. What I would like to know first off is what level are you guys on and when do you plan on getting out of here? Let's take turns, and I'll start over here first with Jay T., and then next time I'll ask you first Josh."
Jay T.:	"I'm on Level 5, but I'll probably get kicked back to a lower level for this fight."
David:	"Is that something you want?"
Jay T.:	"Hell no, uh oh, that will get me a minor. I forgot! If they find out I said hell."
David:	"Well that is a rule you have to watch out for in the real world of the institution, but I have no interest in that. I'm interested if dropping to a lower level is something you want?"
Jay T.:	"Man, are you different. And no, no, I don't want that! That will mean I will just be here a lot longer. Does that mean that you can stop the worker from giving us a major OR for fighting?"
David:	"No. I have no control over whether he does or does not give you both an OR. However, I will be making a report to him on what the two of you decide on doing differently. And I would hazard a guess that if you come up with a plan to stop fighting that will work, the worker will probably take that into consideration. He told me he was waiting to write it until he heard from me, so I would like to give him a very good report. OK? Jay T., you answered the question when you said you don't want to move down to Level Four. Now, Josh, the same question to you. Do you want to go to a lower level, or

	would you rather continue at level four and work toward getting to Level Five where Jay T. is?"
Josh:	"No. I don't want to go back. I want to get out of here as soon as I can. What are you going to tell the worker about us?"
David:	"Well, I don't have anything to tell him yet. I would like to ask a few more questions and then see if you think we have a good report to give him."
Jay T.:	"You are going to let us look at the report?"
David:	"Sure. We are working on this thing together. We can do it."
Jay T.:	"OK. Ask anything you want Dave. Right Josh?"
Josh:	"Yeah, ask away Dave. What we got to lose, huh, Jay T.?"

These responses are a good sign. They are on common ground probably for the first time. I'm encouraged by the positive "want" they are expressing—wanting to continue working toward staying on Level Five for Jay T. and Level Four for Josh, and getting out of the institution eventually. I asked this question to relate to their quality worlds, where they have pictures that are need satisfying.

David:	"Well, since you guys were fighting, I would assume you disagree on some things and are not really very close. In other words, you have a lousy relationship with each other. Now, please answer this question with just a yes or no. Would you say that is a correct assumption? Let's start with you first this time, Josh."
Josh:	"That is right on. He is such a jerk."
David:	"Whoa. Please, just a yes or no. You will get a chance to talk about jerk and other stuff if you want, when we get to that question."
Josh:	"Yes, I'm sorry."
David:	"Sorry? You mean sorry you called Jay T. a jerk?"

I grinned as I said this. I like to use humor in my counseling. When the client responds positively and takes an active part, we are moving in the right direction, which is improving relationships. Remember that humor is part of the fun need that is genetic in all of us. Delinquents, under the control of the law, do not always find much fun in their environment.

Josh: "No. I won't apologize about that."

David: "Jay T., yes or no: do you agree you and Josh have a lousy relationship?"

Jay T. just nodded.

David: "OK, next question. You get this one first Jay T. As a result of our talking today, would you like to improve your relationship with Josh?"

Jay T.:   "What's the purpose? Why would I want to be friends with him?"

David: "I didn't ask you if you wanted to be friends. I asked you if you would like to improve your relationship with him. And as for the purpose, is fighting going to help you get out of this place?"

Jay T.:   "If I have a better relationship with him, will it get me out of here?"

David: "Well, is fighting going to get you out?"

Josh: "I can answer that."

David: "No, no, no, Josh. You will get your turn in just a moment. Now Jay T., do you think if you keep doing what you are doing, fighting with Josh, do you think you will have a very good chance of staying in Level Five and then getting to go home?"

Jay T.:   "No, I guess not."

David: "Then, in order to keep working to get out of here, you would have to do something different from what you've been doing,

	right?" When he nodded, I continued. "Then, would it be helpful or hurtful to improve your relationship with Josh?"
Jay T.:	"Maybe, but he has to improve too."
David:	"We will get this question to him in a moment. Right now, how about you? You said maybe. What does that mean?"
Jay T.:	"Yes, yes. I would be willing to improve it, but I don't know what to do."
David:	"No, we don't know, but we are just trying to explore the possibility of what both of you will be willing to do differently in order to continue your journey on getting out of here."
	"Now Josh, would you be willing to work toward improving your relationship with Jay T.?"
Josh:	"I'll be straight Dave. I don't see any reason to be closer to him because I won't be here in three weeks."
David:	"Will it be three weeks now that you have decided to continue fighting?"
Josh:	"But he pushed me first, and I can prove it!"
Jay T.:	"See, there he is lying again. He ain't goin' home, and I didn't push him first."
David:	"We will cover these complaints in just a few minutes, so please hold them. Now Josh, let's get real man. If you get a bad OR for this last fight, will you be going home in three weeks?"

Both boys were quiet as Josh thought over my questions. This situation is what I have been aiming for, to help both boys self-evaluate, which requires them to do some thinking.

Josh:	"No, I guess not, but how will a better relationship with this jerk make it any better?"
Dave:	"What do you think? If you fight or if you have a better relationship? Which will help give you a better chance of going home?"

Josh:	"Relationship, I guess, but I don't like the idea of being friends with him."
David:	"As I told Jay T., we are not talking about being friends. We are talking about a better relationship. Will you be willing to work toward a better relationship?"

This process takes a lot of patience. The process is a learning process.

Josh:	(Squirming in his chair.) "Yes, if I don't have to talk with him."
David:	"Do you like to fish?"

Both boys stared at me in disbelief. I like to use metaphors in my counseling, especially when things start dragging or if I want to reinforce the idea of new thinking.

Josh:	"Yeah, I like to fish, but what does that have to do with any thing?"
David:	"Well, Josh, if you were going fishing, would you throw your hook in the water without any bait on it?"
Josh:	"Of course not. That's stupid."
David:	"Well, that's kind of like trying to have a better relationship with someone by never talking to him or her."
Josh:	"Oh, I see what you mean. But it's fun to fish. It won't be fun with this other stuff."
David:	"If it means you have a better chance of getting out of here, is it worth it?"
Josh:	"Yeah, I guess so."
David:	"Guess so?"
Josh:	"All right, all right, yes."
David:	"Then what is your answer?"
Josh:	"I forgot the question."

David: "In order to continue working toward getting to go home for good, are you willing to improve the relationship you have with Jay T?"

Josh: "OK. But I don't know what you want me to do."

David: "I'm going to be very honest with you guys. If neither one of you agreed to work on improving the relationship between you, I would have to admit to the worker that we're getting nowhere. You both answered the last question in a manner that allows us to continue. I have four more questions for both of you and if you can answer each one of them to my satisfaction, I can help you guys with your report to the worker. If you miss any of the next four questions, I can't help you, and you will have to suffer whatever consequences are in place."

I waited a moment to let the boys process this information. Then, I continued by teaching some Choice Theory.

"Now, next question. It's your turn to go first Josh. In order to make the relationship better, whose behavior can you control to do that?"

Josh: "Huh? What do ya mean?"

David: "OK Josh, in order for the relationship to get better between you guys, whose behavior can you control? Can you control what Jay T. does."

Josh: "Oh, I see what you mean. Just me I guess. I can beat him up maybe."

David: "And if you beat him up, will that get you home, or just more time here?"

Josh: "More time, I know that, I don't want that so I won't beat him up."

David: "So, whose behavior can you control?"

Josh: "All right. Mine. Are you happy?"

David:	"Now Jay T., same question. Whose behavior can you control in order to make the relationship between you guys better?"
Jay T.:	"Just mine, I suppose. What does that have to do with anything?"
David:	"Well, let me answer you this way. If you guys continue to do what you have been doing, do you think there is much chance you are going home anytime soon?"
Jay T.:	"Oooooh. No, not much chance. We have to get along better don't we?"
David:	"No. Either or both of you can continue to do what you've been doing. Fighting, arguing, calling each other names, whatever. It's your choice. It's your life and your choice as to what will help you get out of here and back to your home."
Josh :	"OK. Give us another question; let's get on with it."
David:	"Third question. You get this one first Jay T. You guys have been waiting for this one. Jay T., tell me two things you think Josh does that is really bad for a relationship between the two of you? And Josh, you will be getting the same question."

I limit the complaints to a definite number, otherwise we can get bogged down with the deadly habits that destroy relationships.

Jay T.:	Rubs his hands together and grins. "He is the biggest liar on the campus. You can't trust him, and he talks behind every one's back."
David:	"OK, that's a couple of things, that's all I need. Now Josh what are a couple of things you think are wrong with Jay T. that destroys your relationship with each other?"
Josh:	"He really is a jerk! He turns other people against me and is always giving that better than anyone else crap."
David:	I interrupted. "You both have done a great job of answering that question. In fact, I think it was kind of fun for you guys wasn't it?"

They both nodded and grinned.

> David: "Now the questions really begin to get harder. Do you guys think you are up to it?"

I am again putting them on the same team, which is a little connecting. This situation lets them experience some belonging with each other, maybe for the first time. I am also catering to their power and freedom needs. In addition, the boys seem to be having a little fun. The four genetic psychological needs are covered: the need to belong and be loved, the need for power, the need for freedom, and the need for fun.

> Jay T.: "We can handle anything you dish out."
>
> Josh: "Yeah, fire away, we can answer anything you can come up with."
>
> David: "Good, good. I'm glad you guys are so confident. Here it is. Josh you get this one first. Tell me one thing good about Jay T., and you'll be getting the same question Jay T., so you can be thinking about it. Take your time, we have plenty of that."
>
> Josh: Josh's brow furrowed, and he put his head down and stared at the floor. "Wow, that is hard."
>
> David: "That's OK. Take your time. Name one good thing about Jay T."

Several seconds passed.

> Josh: "He will always answer any question I have. Sometimes he is wrong, but he will answer you and not ignore anyone."
>
> David: "OK. Very good. Now Jay T., name one good thing about Josh."
>
> Jay T.: "He dresses pretty good."
>
> David: "That is good, but can you tell me something about him as a person that is good?"

Several more seconds passed.

Jay T.:   "He can be trusted to do what he says he will."

David: "Great! You guys did a great job with that question. Now it really gets tough. Are you ready for the last question?"

The boys looked at each other, then both nodded, and no words were spoken.

                "I'll start with you Jay T. This is Monday. What will you do between now and Friday, Jay T., that will make this relationship between you and Josh better?"

Jay T.:   He stared at the floor. "I could not fight with him."

David: "That will be fine, but telling me something you won't do isn't that helpful. I need to know what you will be willing to do to make the relationship better. One thing on an ongoing basis."

Almost a minute elapsed.

Jay T.:   "I could tell him that his word is good, instead of calling him a liar."

David: "Are you saying you will compliment Josh on positive things that you see during the next four days?"

Jay T.:   "Yeah, I'll do that. I have never done that."

David: "We know you haven't done that, but this is a good thing you have come up with. You are going to compliment Josh, right?"

Jay T.:   "Yes, I can do that."

David: "Now Josh, what is one thing you will do from now through Friday on an ongoing basis to improve the relationship between you and Jay T.?"

Josh thought about this for a moment.

Josh:	"Well, he has been here longer than I have, and there have been times when I would have liked to ask him stuff, but I don't."
David:	"I know you don't, but what can you do specifically the next four days to improve the relationship?"
Josh:	"I will call him by his name instead of jerk and ask him what I need to do to get to Level Five. I will ask his advice. But that will be hard."
David:	"Even if it is hard, is it worth doing if it helps you get out of this place?"
Josh:	"Yeah, yeah, you keep coming back to that. You are pretty good at this, aren't you?"
David:	"Look, you guys came up with the plans to improve your lives. I'm just the go-between. I think you both can fix your own tires in the future. What do you think?"

Neither boy said anything. I continued.

	"Well, here is a tablet, and I'm going to have the worker come in here and each of you can write down what you said you are going to do to improve the relationship between the two of you. If you don't do what each of you said, do you think things will get any better and will you still be at your present level or less?"
Josh:	"We'll do it."
Jay T.:	"If it makes it better, it will be worth it."

I had the worker come in, and I told him we had a report for him in the form of a plan. The four of us worked on the plans.

I checked back with the youth worker from time to time. Both boys kept their plan and in three months, Jay T. was released and went home. Josh made Level

Five in two weeks. Despite their spoken desire to not become friends, the two boys were frequently seen together in deep discussions—often arguing over what was right and what was not, but no more fisticuffs occurred.

Structured Reality Therapy

Glasser developed this process to help him in marriage counseling. He asks five questions, and instructs the couple that if they fail to answer any of the questions or answers them incorrectly, he cannot help them.

The first thing he asks them is: "What are you here for?" If they answer anything other than to get marriage counseling, he tells them he can't help them.

Next, he asks them, "Whose behavior can you control in order to make the marriage better?" The third question is: "What do each of you think is wrong with the marriage?" There is a lot of complaining, blaming and other deadly habits used while they respond to this request.

The fourth question is: "What is something good about your spouse?" The last question is asked separately: "What will you do in the following week to make the marriage better?"

The process used with Josh and Jay T. is adapted from the above structured Reality Therapy. The first question David directed to them is about their relationship with each other. David related their success in bettering the relationship to what they want in terms of getting out of the institution—improving their levels, or in Jay T.'s case, maintaining his Level Five to get his release. David followed with the question of whose behavior they can control, then the blaming question, and the one good thing. Finally, he asked the value question of what will each youth be willing to do for a determinate number of days to make the relationship better. This example shows how Glasser's structured Reality Therapy for marriage counseling can be adapted to other relationship problems.

Summary

We all have the need to survive, reproduce, belong, and love, and the need for power, freedom, and fun. Our needs are our ultimate source of motivation. They are general and universal. Within a juvenile facility, the need for power is the most difficult for youth to satisfy. Youth can learn to satisfy the need if staff teach Choice Theory to the juveniles by:

- Asking for their permission
- Asking for their input
- Allowing them to make choices, whenever possible

Questions

1. List the five basic needs that all of us have.

   - _____

   - _____

   - _____

   - _____

   - _____

2. List the one physiological need.

   _____

3. One of the hardest needs to meet in socially approved ways in a juvenile facility is the need for _____.

4. How did David, in the Josh and Jay T. scenario, help the two juveniles satisfy their power needs?

_____

_____

_____

5. The ____ ___ ____ appears to be unique to our species.

6. Our need for power may cause direct conflict with our need to _____.

7. _____ is so basic a need that people will give up their life fighting for it.

8. The day we stop playing is the day we stop _____.

9. _____ are our ultimate source of motivation.

10. ____ are _____ and universal.

11. True/False. According to Glasser, our needs are genetic.

12. True/False. Our behavior is the way we choose to meet our needs.

 # Choice Theory

Objectives

After reading this chapter, you will be able to:

- Identify the four components of Choice Theory
- List the 10 axioms of Choice Theory

Introduction

To fully understand Choice Theory, you must understand basic needs, the quality world, total behavior, and the creative system. In this chapter, we will discuss the new psychology of personal freedom.

Choice Theory

Choice Theory provides the theoretical basis for the practice of Reality Therapy. When we discuss Choice Theory, we must discuss:

- Basic needs, which we did in Chapter 2
- Your quality world, which we will discuss in Chapter 4
- Total behavior, which we will discuss in Chapter 5
- Your creative system, which we will discuss in Chapter 6

- A new psychology of personal freedom, which is the topic of this chapter. You will realize personal freedom when you use Choice Theory to live your life.

While it provides the framework for Reality Therapy, Choice Theory does not tell us what to say. Certain things, however, can be eliminated as topics of discussion based on the philosophy of Choice Theory.

1. There is no need to probe at length for the problem. It is always an unsatisfying present relationship.
2. Because the problem is always in the present, there is no need to make a long, intensive investigation into the juvenile's past. The one exception is when the youth has behaved in a manner that has solved the same problem he or she is now having. We would ask the youth: "Are you willing to try that behavior again?"
3. In traditional counseling, a lot of time is spent both inquiring into and listening to juveniles complain about: their symptoms, the actions of other people, the world they live in, and on and on, the list is endless. Complaining is an effort to avoid talking about the real problem of relationships. We can immediately address the real problem—what the juveniles are choosing to do now.

As Glasser points out: "… finding the present relationship, avoiding the past and excessive complaints about the present, and sticking to what clients can do, not only shortens therapy, it also helps clients understand that they are free to lead more effective lives." (Glasser, *Choice Theory*)

The subtitle of Choice Theory is "A New Psychology of Personal Freedom." The personal freedom comes from giving up external control in our relationships with others. Choice Theory is based on the following beliefs.

- External control harms everyone, both the controllers and the controlled.
- The only person we can really control is ourselves.

- All living creatures are internally motivated.
- We choose everything we do.
- Our choices are our best attempts to satisfy our needs.
- Unsatisfying relationships (between lovers, husband-wife, parent-child, teacher-student, manager-worker) are the cause of most problems.
- Unless we can improve these relationships, we will have little success in reducing any of the problems—of crime, child abuse, spousal abuse, alcohol and drug addiction and other relationship problems—facing mankind.
- Taking more effective control means making better choices as you relate to others.
- To achieve and maintain the relationships we need, we must stop choosing to coerce, force, compel, punish, reward, manipulate, boss, motivate, criticize, blame, complain, nag, badger, rank, rate, and withdraw.
- We must replace these destructive behaviors with choosing to care, listen, support, negotiate, encourage, love, befriend, trust, accept, welcome, and esteem.

The following words identify the difference between external control psychology and Choice Theory.

External Control Psychology

coerce, compel, punish, reward, manipulate, boss, motivate, criticize, blame, complain, nag, badger, rank, and withdraw

Choice Theory

care, listen, support, negotiate, encourage, love, befriend, trust, accept, welcome, and cooperate

Additional differences between external control and Choice Theory are found in the following chart.

COMPETING VIEWS OF THE WORLD

External Control Psychology
The oldest and most "common sense" way of life, still used by most of the today, world is a universal psychology.

Choice Theory
The relatively new and evolving explanation for how and why we behave as explained by Dr. Glasser.

EXTRINSIC PSYCHOLOGY VS. CHOICE THEORY

Our realities are the same.
The old extrinsic psychology believes that there is one reality.

Our realities are separate.
Choice Theory believes that reality differs for each of us. Our reality is based on how we perceive the information we receive through our sensory systems and how we process it. That's why two people may read the same book, and one likes it, and the other does not.

Everybody sees the same pictures.

The extrinsic psychology believes that we all see the same thing.

Everybody has different pictures.
Choice Theory says that we see the each have different pictures in our quality world. We put into our photo album the pictures that satisfy one or more of our basic needs. We remove those things from our quality world that have ceased to satisfy our needs. These may include parents, teachers, and previous loved ones.

Note: Removing a picture without replacing it with another picture is difficult. Juveniles often will replace pictures with violence, drugs, and unloving sex to get immediate gratification.

EXTRINSIC PSYCHOLOGY VS. CHOICE THEORY (cont'd)

People should be converted to its point of view.
External control tries to convert people. External control tries to coerce, control, and manipulate by compelling, punishing, and rewarding.

People should be persuaded to its point of view.
Choice Theory attempts to persuade. Choice Theory tries to negotiate and compromise without criticizing or complaining, and it tries to do so by listening, caring, and supporting.

I can control others.
1) I can make them do what is right.
2) I must make them do what I want them to because it is the "right" to do.

I can't control others.
Choice Theory says that the only person I can control is myself. You cannot make people do something that they don't want to do, feel something that they don't want to feel, or think something that they don't want to think.

Coercion is practiced when persuasion fails.
In an externally controlled world, the system is naturally coercive. When persuasion (if used at all) fails, coercion is used. When one type of punishment doesn't work, a harder punishment is used. It is like pouring gasoline on a fire.

Collaboration and consensus create new options.
Choice Theory works on collaboration. You may not totally agree with the solution, but you can live with and support it. Each person has the freedom to satisfy his or her basic needs.

Resources are limited.

External control people have limited resources that are mainly centered around control. Once people choose to coerce, punish, reward to control, boss—and all the other deadly habits—the cycle of destructive and relationship destroying behavior becomes never ending.

Resources are unlimited.

Choice Theory, by using caring habits, helps people to connect with each other. When they are closer and have better relationships, people's resources for living happily are unlimited.

There is a minimum degree freedom.

There is less freedom in a naturally coercive system. An excellent example of this is the Berlin Wall that separated Germany (constructed in 1961).

There is a maximum degree of of freedom.

In Choice Theory, there is a maximum degree of freedom. We saw this once the Berlin Wall was torn down (in 1989).

This is a win/lose model.

With external control, one person has to be in control. There always will be a winner and a loser—those with power and those without it.

This is a win/win model.

Choice Theory enables everyone to satisfy his or her need for power. Everyone wins when coercion is eliminated from the relationship.

Choice Theory provides us with 10 axioms that redefine our personal freedom. You have read about them in earlier chapters, and you will see them come alive again and again in later chapters. The 10 axioms of Choice Theory are:

- **The only person whose behavior we can control is our own.**
  Once we realize that the only person we can control is ourselves, we begin to redefine our personal freedom. And, we immediately realize that

we have more freedom than we thought. No one can make us do anything we don't want to do. Similarly, we can't make people do anything they don't want to do. Think how much time you spend trying to make people do something they don't want to do—or how much time you spend resisting doing something someone else wants you to do that you don't want to do. Giving up external control means that you will be able to spend that amount of time in more meaningful interactions with others.

- **All we can give or get from other people is information. How we deal with that information is a choice.**
  As you read the scenarios in this workbook, you will see that we give information to the youth, but what they do with it is up to them. We are responsible for finding ways to present the information so that it is not coercive, punishing, manipulating, criticizing, blaming, complaining, or nagging. When staff give up choosing to coerce youth to accept and/or deal with information, both the staff and the youth regain personal freedom.

- **All long-lasting psychological problems are relationship problems.**
  Choice Theory believes that the cause of our misery is always our way of dealing with an important relationship; it is not working out the way we want it to work out. Our personal freedom is renewed when we do not waste time looking at all other aspects of our lives for why we are choosing misery.

- **The problem relationship is always part of our present lives.**
  We do not need to look to the past or the future to find the problem relationship; it is always a current one. In looking at relationships, we cannot just consider what we want. We also must consider what the other person wants. We must find ways to meet our needs in such a way that we do not deny the other person from satisfying his or her needs. This choice is not totally free, and our personal freedom is redefined when we realize that the needs of both the other person and ourselves must be satisfied.

- **What happened in the past that was painful has a great deal to do with what we are today. But revisiting this painful past can**

contribute little or nothing to what we need to do now: improve an important, present relationship.

What is over is over. We cannot be a prisoner of what has happened, what cannot be changed. It is no way to gain personal freedom. We can enjoy reliving the satisfying things in our past. But we must free ourselves of the idea that we must understand the past to deal with the present relationship.

- **We are driven by five genetic needs: survival and reproduction, love and belonging, power, freedom, and fun.**

Needs can be delayed but not denied. Others can help us satisfy our needs, and we can help others satisfy their needs. But deciding when our needs are satisfied is up to each one of us. Only we can decide when these needs are satisfied. No one can decide that for us. Similarly, we cannot decide when someone else's needs are satisfied.

- **We can satisfy our needs only by satisfying the pictures in our quality world.**

We all have pictures in our quality world that we try to satisfy. We give up freedom when we have pictures in our quality world that we cannot satisfy. One example is when we put a million dollar house in our quality world when we cannot afford it. Therefore, what we choose to put into our quality world is important.

- **All we can do from birth to death is behave.**

Choice Theory believes that all behavior is total behavior and is made up of four inseparable components: acting, thinking, feeling, and physiology.

- **All total behavior is designated by verbs, usually infinitives (the "to" form of a verb—e.g., I would like to talk [infinitive] to you) and gerunds (the "ing" form of a verb when it acts as a noun—e.g., Walking [gerund] in the rain is fun), and named by the component that is most recognizable.**

- **All total behavior is chosen but we have arbitrary control over only the acting and thinking components. We can, however, control our feelings and physiology indirectly through how we choose to act and think.**

58

We can directly control our acting and thinking. By doing so, we indirectly control our feelings and our physiology. Understanding this concept allows us to be free to control what we can control and avoid what we cannot control. Our personal freedom is enhanced as we experience greater satisfaction in our acting and thinking.

Summary

In summary, we would like to quote William Glasser as he stresses the importance of personal freedom and the axioms of Choice Theory.

"Whenever you feel as if you don't have the freedom you want in a relationship, it is because you, your partner, or both of you are unwilling to accept the choice theory axiom: *You can only control your own life.* Until you learn this axiom, you will not be able to use any of the choice theory ideas such as basic needs, the quality world, and total behavior. But once you learn it, all of the choice theory becomes accessible to you. You can then freely choose to move closer to the people you want to be close with no matter how they behave. But the more they, too, learn choice theory, the better you will get along with them. Choice theory supports the golden rule. To gain the freedom to use it is the purpose of this book." (Glasser, *Choice Theory*) So be it for this workbook as well.

Questions

1. List the key parts of Choice Theory.

    * _____

    * _____

    * _____

    * _____

    * _____

2. List three things that can be eliminated as topics of discussion in Choice Theory.

- _____

- _____

- _____

3. Personal freedom comes from giving up _____ _____ in our relationships with others.

4. The only _____ whose behavior we can control is ___ ___.

5. List the 10 axioms of Choice Theory.

- _____

- _____

- _____

- _____

- _____

- _ _____

- _____

- _____

- _____

- _____

CHAPTER 4

Quality World

Objectives

After reading this chapter, you will be able to:

- List the three classifications of things we put into our quality world
- Discuss how drugs, unloving sex, violent crime, and alcohol are in some people's quality world

We already have discussed basic needs and the new psychology of personal freedom. In this chapter, we will discuss your quality world, and how you choose to put in and take out of your quality world people, things and ideas.

Your Quality World

Shortly after birth, we begin to develop a small personal world that is unique to each of us. This quality world is like a photo album, where we store those pictures (perceptions) that satisfy our needs—the four psychological needs of power, love and belonging, fun, and freedom, as well as the one physiological need of survival and reproduction. Our mother is most likely the first picture we put into our quality world. Throughout our life, we continue to create and re-create this unique personal world. In each of our quality worlds are the:

- people we most want to be with
- things we most want to own or experience
- ideas or systems of belief that govern much of our behavior

Therefore, we learn that we feel much better when we are with other people, have particular things, take certain actions, or follow certain beliefs. If we succeed in satisfying a picture in our quality world, we experience joy. One or more of our basic needs have been met. Anytime we do not succeed in satisfying a picture in our quality world, we experience unhappiness. Advertisers may not know about quality worlds, but they try to play to our quality world with their ads.

Advertisers are clever at appealing to our (adults and especially juveniles) quality worlds. For example, restaurants flaunt the "All You Can Eat" ads to draw customers. This enticement appeals to our need for:

- survival—having a chance to eat (we must eat)
- power—getting more for our money and achieving success in more purchasing power for our dollar
- freedom—looking at the many items that we can choose
- fun—experiencing joy in selecting food items that taste so good to our pallets
- love and belonging—being with people and making new acquaintances

Restaurants would like for us to add these pictures to our quality world.

Another example is the ads for cars. For instance, Chevrolet's ad "Like a Rock" addresses our need for power (own a strong, reliable vehicle), need for love and belonging (share the vehicle with a family member), and fun (ride through the mountains or just about anywhere).

But not all ads are seen as positive. Cigarette and beer manufactures have been criticized for allegedly targeting juveniles in ads. The character Joe Camel, for example, apparently appealed to juveniles' needs for love and belonging, power, fun, and freedom. The pictures in the juveniles' photo album supposedly would include smoking Camels and having lots of friends, fun, and freedom. Consequently, Joe Camel was removed from the ads. Interestingly, the "Marlboro Man" appears to have power, lots of freedom, and fun riding horses. Therefore, he could be criticized as well for appealing to juveniles.

When beer ads are shown are television, the beer sometimes isn't even mentioned until the closing frame. The ads usually sell fun, freedom, power, and lots of love and belonging. Some people actually watch the Super Bowl (professional football championship) to see the new beer ads, rather than to watch the game. The ads often are discussed at work with laughter the next day.

All advertisers, therefore, are trying to get their "product" into our quality world. They want us to believe that if we just use their product, we can meet many of our needs.

The same can be said of musicians. Look at the musicians that the juveniles you supervise like. What is the musicians' appeal? How did they get in the juveniles' quality world? Do they appeal to the need to be loved and to belong? Power? Freedom? Fun? Survival? You probably will find that the musicians appeal to most, if not all, the basic needs.

Parents, teachers, and juvenile careworkers are added to or removed from juvenile offenders' quality world because of relationships and interactions. Someone once said that parents are "consultants to their kids" and, like all consultants, they can be fired at any time. The same can be said of teachers and juvenile careworkers. Our pictures can be removed quickly from juveniles' picture album if our relationship with them is based on any of the deadly habits—criticizing, blaming, complaining, threatening, punishing, nagging, and rewarding to control.

We define our quality world, our reality, in the way it works best for us, regardless of what other people say. If you see a movie and it fits with your quality world, you will enjoy it regardless of what others may say about the movie. If you fall in love with someone who fits the image in your quality world, what your family and friends think of the person does not matter. What counts is what you think.

Some examples may help make this point clearer. Imagine being in a room where the thermostat is set on 72 degrees. You feel cold, and the person next to you feels warm. The temperature is 72 degrees, which is a fact or reality. However, reality for you is that it's cold, and reality for the person next to you is that it's warm.

After the tragedies of September 11, 2001 in our country, many people removed the picture of flying from their quality world. They replaced it with a picture of driving or taking a train.

Ewing Kauffman, prior owner of the Kansas City Royals baseball team, once attended West Port Junior High School. In a speech to a graduating class, he made a pledge to the students: "If you graduate from high school, do not use drugs, and are not a parent prior to graduation, I will pay for you to attend the college of your choice." Mr. Kauffman was amazed and disappointed that 100 percent of the students did not take him up on his pledge. A picture of going to college was neither in the quality world of some students nor in the quality world of their parents. They did not think it was possible, even after he pledged to pay for it. His pledge did not place the picture of going to college into their quality worlds. Mr. Kauffman hired people to work with the students (build relationships) on their grades, goals, esteem, and with their parents in providing support for their children. By building relationships, he increased the number of students who accepted his pledge.

Most of us are happy and have a number of people in our quality world. These people usually include our family members, loved ones and at least one friend. Many juvenile offenders do not have anyone in their quality world. They have not found anyone they enjoy being with and can trust. They have been abused, deserted and rejected. They have removed parents, teachers, others and school from their quality world. To feel good, they replace the people pictures with non-people pictures such as drugs, unloving sex, crime, and violence.

This point is best illustrated by gang members. All of us have experienced unhappiness at times. Most of us are connected to family and friends and gain support to help us through those unhappy times. Such support demonstrates the importance of meeting the need for love and belonging. Because gang members do not have this support, they combat their unhappiness by finding immediate pleasure in violence, drugs, and unloving sex. Staff working with youth who are gang members face the challenge of persuading (we cannot make people do anything they do not want to do) them to replace wrong pictures with right ones. Staff can help the juveniles learn how to connect in a loving way through a positive relationship with adults and other people outside the gang. To be successful, staff must model caring behavior and avoid the deadly habits that destroy relationships.

Let's look at how David teaches Choice Theory to Tommie and tries to persuade him to change the pictures in his quality world. Tommie, age 16, has been referred to the juvenile court twice. For the first offense of theft, he was sent home to his parents. For the second offense of using drugs, he was placed on probation. David has seen Tommie once a week over a six-week duration. This meeting is the seventh one.

David: "Hi Tommie, it's good to see you. How are your pictures this morning?"

I always greet a juvenile or his parents with a positive attitude, which often is contagious. Prior to this meeting with Tommie, we have spent a great deal of time getting to know each other. I have shared some things in my quality world, those things that are need satisfying (such as seeing my grandchildren and gardening), with Tommie to build trust. Consequently, Tommie has connected with me to the extent he feels comfortable in sharing some of his quality world (no one ever knows everything that is in another person's quality world). Tommie shared with me that he had a picture of owning his own bicycle and pictures of marijuana cigarettes in his quality world. He had rather quickly picked up the concepts of the quality world as I shared Choice Theory with him. Once he grasped the ideas, I began greeting him the way that I did on the seventh meeting.

Tommie:	"Pictures could be better. They are bummers today."
David:	"I'm sorry to hear that, want to share with me? Maybe I can help."
Tommie:	"I have this picture of wanting to steal another bicycle, and maybe some other stuff out of this old man's garage just down the street from my house."
David:	"How long have you had these pictures in your quality world?"
Tommie:	"It started last Saturday when I saw him open his garage door, and I could see all the stuff he has in there. He is like an old pack rat, and he will never use it. He probably wouldn't even miss the stuff, especially that bicycle."
David:	"Why didn't you steal it?"
Tommie:	"I don't know. I just didn't."
David:	"Are you planning on it?"
Tommie:	"If I was, what would you do."
David:	"I would ask you not to, and we would talk about other pictures you might substitute for that crap. You know what I mean?"
Tommie:	"Yeah, yeah, yeah. I know. But it's hard because I need some dough to buy a joint, and I really do want that bicycle."
David:	"If you had the bicycle, would you still have the picture of a joint?"
Tommie:	"I'll always have the picture of a joint, but then I have a picture of the boys' reform school too. I don't know what to do. They are both in my quality world."

David:	"Tommie, there is never anything negative in our quality worlds, so the reform school is in a different place in your head than your quality world. It is in the place where we keep all the information we ever received. All our experiences in life. Then we take those best things and put them in our quality world. Those things that satisfy those five needs we talked about earlier. Remember?"
Tommie:	"Oh yeah, now I remember. Well, how come that picture of pot is in my quality world?"
David:	"Because it makes you feel good. All drugs make you feel good for awhile. But then when it becomes a downer, it does not feel so good. Right?"
Tommie:	"Yeah, but what can I do?"
David:	"Well, you said if you had a bicycle, you would feel better. So, let's talk about how you can get a bicycle legally."
Tommie:	"I could get a job at Price Chopper or IGA. They always need someone after school to stock and clean up and other stuff. But I don't want to work."
David:	"Look Tommie. I can't make you work, or anything else, but I have an opinion. Are you interested? If not, just tell me, and I won't waste your time."
Tommie:	"No, I would like to hear your opinion."
David:	"Well, the reality of the situation is that if you get caught doing pot or any other drug, the judge will most likely send you to the reform school or some other facility for juveniles. You have already told me earlier that is something you do not want. Is that correct?"
Tommie:	"Yeah, I don't want to be taken from my home and the school I go to."
David:	"Well, it makes sense to me that it would be in your best interest to do what you have to in order to put some new pictures into your quality world in order to get that bicycle and get to live at home. Would you agree with that?"

Tommie:	"But I don't want to have to get a job."
David:	"Tommie, you don't have to. It is your choice on where you want to live and go to school. I can only guarantee you that the judge will not take you away from your home if you don't break the law again. That means you could relax and not be looking over your shoulder every time you stop outside your home. You can choose to get a job at Price Chopper or wherever, save your money, and buy a bike, or you can keep on doing what you have been doing and keep watching out for the cops. Is that something you want for the rest of your life?"
Tommie:	"NO! I don't want that. O.K. I'll put my application in at the Chopper."
David:	"When will you do that, Tommie?"
Tommie:	"Oh … next week."
David:	"What's the matter with today?"
Tommie:	"Oh, I'm supposed to meet some friends and cruise the mall."
David:	"Why can't you do both?"
Tommie:	"O.K. O.K. Daddy David Do Good, I'll do it. Can I leave early so I can do that?"
David:	"You've got me pal. But I want to know tomorrow how it went. Call me during your lunch break at school, O.K.?"
Tommie:	"Yeah, I'll call. Thanks Dave. Thanks for helping me get better pictures."

Anorexia is a graphic example of the strength of the quality world and how the wrong pictures can ruin lives. Before she died, singer Karen Carpenter had become so thin and undernourished that audiences gasped when they saw her come on stage.

We can only speculate what pictures were in the quality worlds of entertainers Elvis and John Belushi, who died of drug overdoses. We know that famous people may become isolated from meaningful relationships. Individuals without meaningful relationships, whether famous or not, either begin to doubt or have found out that they cannot trust some people. Such individuals replace people pictures with nonpeople pleasure pictures—pictures of unloving sex, alcohol, drugs and even violent crime—in their quality world. They have no one to trust, but they want to feel good, as we all want to feel good. They turn to what is available to them, usually drugs, sex, and/or alcohol. These individuals can fool their brains with these nonpeople pictures because they produce feelings similar to those produced when one or more of the individuals' needs is satisfied. However, there is one major problem. Drugs, unloving sex, and alcohol can provide pleasure, but they cannot provide happiness. We need other people in our lives and in our quality worlds to provide us with happiness.

Therefore, we must replace the nonpeople pictures with people pictures. Using Choice Theory and Reality Therapy, we can learn to build relationships and picture ourselves satisfying our needs with other people. Once again, drugs provide pleasure; they cannot provide happiness. For happiness, we need people. Even the character Tom Hanks played in the movie *Castaway* chose to have Wilson—an imaginary person created by painting a face on a soccer ball.

The same is true with things. Most of the things we place into our quality world are associated with people because this attachment provides much of the good feeling we all want and need. We need and want someone with whom to share those things.

What we believe in must be shared with people. Our religion, political convictions and way of life need to be shared with someone else. By themselves, they do not get into our quality world. We feel hurt (pain) when we can't convince someone close to us that our values are important.

Summary

Shortly after birth, we begin to develop a small personal world that is unique to each of us. In this world, we put in people we most want to be with; things we most want to have; and ideas or beliefs that govern much of our behavior. The people, things and ideas we choose are those with which we feel better when we are with them. They tend to either fulfill our needs or to fool our brains into producing the feelings that are similar to how we feel when a need is satisfied.

Questions

1. List the three classifications of things we find in our quality world.

   _____

   _____

   _____

2. How do we choose to put these people, things or ideas into our quality world?

   _____

   _____

3. We can fool our brains with _____ pleasure pictures that produce feelings which are similar to how we feel when any need is satisfied.

4. Drugs can provide _____; they cannot provide _____.

5. For happiness, we need _____ in our lives.

CHAPTER 5

 # Total Behavior

Objectives

After reading this chapter, you will be able to:

- Explain total behavior
- List the four components that make up our total behavior
- Explain what you need to do if what you are choosing to do is not satisfying the pictures in your quality world
- Explain why Choice Theory uses the verb form rather than the noun or adjective form

We have discussed basic needs, the new psychology of personal freedom, and quality worlds. In this chapter, we will discuss total behavior. All we can do from birth until death is behave. Our total behavior is made up of acting, thinking, feeling and the physiology that goes along with them. We behave in a way that gives us the most effective control over our lives. If what we are choosing to do is not satisfying the pictures in our quality world, we have three choices. We can choose to change what we want, change what we are doing, or both.

Total Behavior

According to Choice Theory:

- All we can do from birth to death is **behave**.
- All behaviors are **total**.
- All behavior is **chosen**.
- All we get from outside of us is **information**.
- The only person's behavior we can control is our **own**.

Our total behavior is made up of four inseparable components working together. The four components that make up our total behavior are:

- Acting
- Thinking
- Feeling
- Physiology

When we hear the word behavior, many of us think of activities such as walking, running, talking, listening, sitting, jumping, and so forth. These are *doing activities*. Acting is the first of the four inseparable components that make up our total behavior.

Some of us do not immediately relate thinking to behavior. Thinking appears to be more passive than acting and is common to us only because we are always thinking about something. Thinking is the second component of our total behavior.

Whenever we behave, we are also always feeling something. We may be glad, sad, mad or experiencing some other feeling. However, we are always feeling something. Feeling is the third component of our total behavior.

The last of the four components that make up our total behavior is our physiology. There is always some physiology associated with all that we are doing. We are breathing deeply, our heart is beating, our palms are sweating, and so forth.

Choice Theory tells us that we have control over our total behavior. We are not only always behaving but also behaving in a way that gives us the most effective control over our lives. This means that we are choosing to behave in a manner that reasonably satisfies the pictures in our quality worlds and that meets our needs.

You may be thinking, "Hey wait a moment. I don't have control over what I feel or what my physiology is." Yet, if you buy into the concept of total behavior, you know that you have direct control over your actions and thoughts. Because our total behavior is all four of the components, then our feeling and physiology are tied to what we are doing and thinking. If we choose to do something that makes us feel good, then we are choosing to feel good. While this may be more indirect control than we have over our actions and thinking, we still exercise indirect control over how we feel.

The same is true if you choose to do something that gives you pain. If you deliberately hit your thumb with a hammer, you have chosen the feeling of pain and the physiology (swelling and bleeding) that goes with your actions.

Choice Theory uses verbs rather than adjectives to describe action. For example, we are depressing (verb) rather than we are depressed (adjective). We actively choose what we are complaining about, and we can learn to make better choices. If we are choosing to depress, therefore, we also can choose to do things so that we will not depress. By changing the way we act and think, we also change the way we feel and our physiology. Our chosen actions and thoughts are inseparable from how we feel and our physiology.

Glasser provides the following scenario to explain total behavior. His neighbor, who is a consistent five-mile-a-day runner, comes up the street toward Glasser's house.

> "Glasser: 'Hey. Come sit on my porch in the shade and have a glass of
>   water.'

The neighbor gladly obliges and has a seat on the steps. Glasser gets him a glass of water and decides to teach him a little Choice Theory.

"Glasser: 'Why are you perspiring so much?'
"Friend: 'I was running. No one can run on a day like this and not perspire; running and sweating go together.'
"Glasser: 'I agree they go together, but why do you say that the running caused the sweating? Why don't you say the sweating caused the running?'
"He, not knowing total behavior, looks at me as if I'm crazy.

"Friend: 'I don't understand what you're driving at.'

"He is so used to external control psychology that what I have said to him is confusing. He is used to thinking that one thing causes the other, but using the same logic, it makes just as much sense to say that sweating causes running. In actual fact, they do go together, neither causes the other. What causes both the running (the acting component) and the sweating (the physiological component) is his choice to run. If he had not chosen to run, he would not be perspiring."

If what we are choosing to do is not satisfying the pictures in our quality worlds, we can choose to do three different things:

- Change what we want
- Change what we are doing
- Change both

The verb form is active and denotes control. To be depressed, anxious, phobic and so forth is passive. Being passive means being helpless, which prevents people from ever thinking that they can do something more than accept their fate. Verbs put us in touch with the core philosophy of Choice Theory: We are choosing what we are doing, but we are capable of choosing something better. The use of verbs in Choice Theory provides hope and direction to change.

Suppose a juvenile is choosing to be upset and to anger over not being released from the facility. You can ask the juvenile how choosing to anger is going to help him get what he wants. If the juvenile still wants the early release, he will have to change what he is doing. The juvenile may have to modify the earliest release date to one that is more realistic and change what he is doing. The goal is to replace external control with internal control.

The following is a scenario with 16-year-old Albert who is having difficulty controlling his anger. First, we will observe Albert "out of control" (in reality, we are never "out of control," we are either in more effective control of our lives or less effective control of our lives). Then, we will see Albert beginning to use internal control for his behavior. When we use the term behavior, we are always referring to total behavior.

Albert dropped his tray of food, spat out some curse words, and picked up the nearest chair and threw it against the wall. Two youth workers quickly escorted Albert to the timeout room. Once inside, Albert began pounding his fist into the padded walls of the room. The workers asked me if I wanted to talk with Albert and "use some of that choice stuff." I said that I would see Albert, but I wanted no one else present during this time. Any other observable people would just interfere with my attempts to reunite with Albert. I had known Albert and talked with him enough that we had formed a fairly good relationship. To keep him from being threatened and for my own protection, I would remain outside the room and initially talk to Albert through the bars.

David: "Albert, I need some advice from you rather quickly, so that's why I'm intruding on your privacy. (Not waiting for a reply, I continue.) The advice I need is when can I talk with you? The workers think you are too upset to see me, but I don't believe that. Whose right?"

Albert: "(He stopped hitting the wall with his fist.) WHAT DO YOU WANT TO SEE ME ABOUT? (He lowered his voice.) I don't want to see nobody … I'll never get out of here."

David: "Well, I can tell you that you are wrong about that. You are 16, and they have never kept any juveniles in here past their 18th birthday. So, you wont' be here forever."

Albert: "It might as well be forever. (He began hitting the padded walls again.)"

David: "I'll make you a bet Albert. I'll bet you I can give you some information that will help you work toward getting out quicker than the direction you are presently going. Interested?"

There was a long pause. Then, Albert slowly turned around and stared at me.

Albert: "Are you jivin' me?"

David: "I don't jive. Ask any of the guys I have seen. And you and I have talked a few times. You are a bright guy; you know whether I'm for real or not. How about it. Can we talk? If you get tired of me, just give me the word, and I'm history. O.K.?"

Albert: "Oh, all right, but I ain't promising anything."

David: "That's fine. I won't ask you to promise anything except one thing."

Albert: "(Suspicious.) What's that?"

David: "That when I come in there you won't mistake me for that padded wall."

Albert grinned, and I knew he was in more effective control. He had started doing and thinking something different; therefore, his feelings were better, and his physiology also had changed. I summoned a worker and had him let me into the timeout room.

David: "Hey, that's better. I hate talking through those bars. Now, what did you want to see me about?"

Albert: "I shouldn't be laughing, but man, you're funny. You said you could tell me something to help me get out of this place, so what is it?"

David:	"Albert, I want you to think of jumping and thinking. O.K.?"
Albert:	"Huh?"
David:	"Come on, go with me on this. Think about jumping and thinking. Tell me when you have thought of them."
Albert:	"I feel silly, but O.K. I thought of them, now what?"
David:	"Now I want you to do something else, ready?"
Albert:	"I don't like this game. It's boring."
David:	"Oh, so you were jivin' me when you said you wanted to work toward getting out of here."
Albert:	"O.K. O.K. I'll play this little game."
David:	"Is it a game to try and get out of here?"
Albert:	"O.K. You've made your point. Go ahead."
David:	"I want you to close your eyes, and when I touch your arm, I want you to immediately jump. O.K. Don't think. Just jump."
Albert:	"Why? I don't understand. I don't want to close my eyes."
David:	"Look, this is serious. I'm going to show you a way to help you get out of here sooner than you otherwise would. I trusted you when I asked your advice about talking to you, now will you trust me? (When he nodded, I continued.) You will understand. Ready?"
Albert:	"(Closing his eyes.) Yeah, go ahead."
	I touched him on the arm. It took a couple of seconds, and then he gave a little jump.
David:	"O.K. What did you think?"
Albert:	"I thought … you told me not to think."
David:	"I know, but isn't it hard not to think before you jump? What did you think?"
Albert:	"I thought, why am I trusting this dude, but if it helps I'll do it."
David:	"I want to ask you a very important question. May I?"

It is obvious that we have a good connection going here, and I am asking his permission to ask another question. Asking people permission is a powerful tool. It helps them meet their power needs. The need for power is one that Albert has great difficulty satisfying without angering.

Albert: "Sure, ask away."

David: "To get out of here earlier than your 18th birthday, are you willing to make a major change in the way you think about things, and even do things?"

Albert: "O.K. Here it comes. The lecture about my anger."

David: "Nope, no lecture, just a question. May I?"

Albert: "Yeah, yeah, go ahead."

David: "Do you think that as long as you continue to anger the way you do that you have any possible chance of getting out of here before you are 18?"

Albert: "No, but I can't help it. They make me angry in this place."

David: "Albert. You didn't jump when I touched you. You thought about it first. You took time to think because it was important to you. Isn't that right?"

Albert looked at me in amazement. I could see the wheels turning as he thought about what I had said.

Albert: "Sure. But how can that help me with my anger? If not getting angry helps me get out, I want to do that. But how?"

David: "Well, first you choose to anger just as you choose to jump. You got the information from me about touching your arm, and you jumped. But, you thought about it. You got information in the cafeteria when you dropped your tray. And you chose to throw the chair. You chose. Now if you will think about getting out of here instead of thinking anger, you can learn to control your life much better, if that is what you want. What do you think?"

Albert just shook his head. He stared at me and then looked at his hands. His confusion was obvious.

Albert:	"But how can I remember to think? It just happens."
David:	"Well, maybe you need a reminder. Would you be interested in a reminder?"
Albert:	"What's a reminder?"
David:	"Something that would help remind you to think, because there is nothing wrong with your thinking, is there?"
Albert:	"No, but how can I remember?"
David:	"I have a suggestion, if you are interested."
Albert:	"Yeah, yeah. Anything that will help me get out of here."
David:	"Ask the workers to say a word to you when they see you starting to choose to anger."
Albert:	"What word?"
David:	"What word do you think would help you think?"
Albert:	"(Grinning.) THINK!"

In team meetings, Albert worked with the youth workers to help him with his "reminder word." In addition, some of his peers began to help him as well as the workers and counselors. It took time, but eventually, Albert made excellent progress on controlling his anger and was released prior to his 18th birthday.

Once the juvenile learns he can control his behavior, he can apply internal control to different situations. He knows that he can change what he wants, change his behavior or both. For example, suppose the juvenile is choosing to anger because of not getting a date. He can give himself this little speech: "I am choosing to anger because I didn't get a date. How is this choice of anger going to help me deal with this situation? If it isn't helping me, can I choose to do something better?"

Some people have difficulty with the concept of choosing their behaviors. For example, who would choose to feel miserable, that is, choose the bad feeling of depressing. Glasser isn't saying we choose our feelings. To the contrary, he is saying we choose a total behavior that includes all four components, of which the feeling component of depression is present. Because we name the total behavior by its most observable component, we call that total behavior depressing. Similarly, walking is named after the most obvious component, acting, which in this case is the action of walking. The same goes for any total behavior, whether it is pondering (thinking) our next move, vomiting (physiology), headaching (feeling), running (action) and so on.

When you're teaching the concept of total behavior to youth, you can use an excellent metaphor developed by Glasser: the car. He uses the four wheels of the car to illustrate how the four components of total behavior work together. The front wheels of the car are the acting and thinking components. The two back wheels are the physiology and feeling components. The two front wheels determine which direction our car (behavior) will go. If a youth chooses to steal a car, he has steered his total behavior down the "steal a car road."

Of course, when the two front wheels go in a certain direction, the back wheels, physiology and feelings, follow along. This fact is important because by changing our acting and thinking (the only components that we can arbitrarily change), we can change our feelings and physiology. That is why asking the juvenile "How do you feel" is not particularly helpful. We can't change our feelings without first changing our actions and thinking. If the opposite were true, we could merely say, "Cheer up." And, the counseling process could be reduced to mere external directions. We have learned that statements such as "Straighten up young man," "You better get your act together," and so forth have no influence on improving unacceptable behavior. Therefore, in counseling, asking questions directed at the acting and thinking components is most helpful: "What are you going to *do* about your situation?" "What do you *think* you could do differently to keep out of trouble?"

Observing the behavior of a juvenile can be helpful in determining which components are in operation as the youth behaves. The following is a short description of a youth behaving. As you read it, write down the components that you think you can recognize. If you're not sure, make an educated guess on what you might be occurring. You can check your answer on page 253.

Jerry watched the store for awhile and when he decided no one was looking, he entered through the side door. He stopped and looked at the unattended cash register, then scurried to it and breathlessly struggled to force it open. His heart was pounding, and he was dismayed that the drawer would not pop open. His anxiety quickly was overtaking his reasoning. Suddenly, the drawer popped open, and he saw hundreds of twenty dollar bills just waiting for him to scoop them up. His mouth was dry as he drew in his breath and realized that if he was caught, he would be sent to prison. His thoughts raced: "Since I'm on probation, I better do something differently. Or, I'm going to make a very bad choice and go to the slammer." He chose to change his actions and walked away, all the while thinking that this action was not what he wanted to do. But it would be better in the long run. His feelings were of relief, and his heart began to beat more regularly as he exited the door.

Another exercise that is helpful is to look at what you would ordinarily say using external control and change it into internal control language. For example:

Probation Officer: **External Control Language**
"Well, I checked up on you with your mother, and she informs me you broke your curfew last night. It's back to court for you and a revocation of your probation. You are history!"

Probation Officer: **Choice Theory Language (internal control language)**
"Your mother and I are very concerned about you. Let's talk about the probation rules the court set out. I know it is difficult to change from what you are used to doing, but what can we work out together to help you keep the rules set out by the judge? What do you think?"

Now it's your turn. Change the following language from external control to internal control. You can check your answers on page 254.

A. Youth Worker: "I am sick and tired of yelling at you about keeping your room cleaned up. I'm giving you paper (bad observation report), and you will end up at level one."

Youth Worker: _____

_____

_____

B. Youth Worker: "Look at this mess. You can't do anything right, can you?!"

Youth Worker: _____

_____

_____

C. Youth Worker: "Late, late, late. You're constantly late. What is your problem?"

Youth Worker: _____

_____

_____

D. Youth Worker: "I'll tell you what. You knock off the behavior, and you just might get to see the movie tonight."

Youth Worker: _____

_____

_____

Summary

Our total behavior has four interrelated parts—acting, thinking, feeling, and physiology. We have direct control over our actions and thoughts; we have indirect control over our feelings and physiology. We choose to behave in a way that satisfies the pictures in our quality world.

Questions

1. All we can do from birth until death is _____.

2. The four components that make up our total behavior are:

   • _____

   • _____

   • _____

   • _____

3. If what we are choosing to do is not satisfying the pictures in our quality world, what can we do?

   _____

   _____

   _____

4. Why does Choice Theory use the verb form rather than the noun or adjective form?

   _____

   _____

   _____

5. The use of verbs in Choice Theory provides _____ and _____ to change.

6. Questions directed toward the _____ and _____ components are most helpful in working with youth.

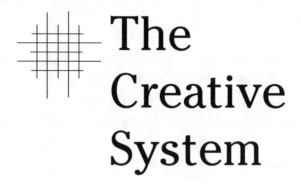 # The Creative System

Objectives

After reading this chapter, you will be able to:

- Explain our creative system
- Give two examples of our creative systems in action

To fully understand Choice Theory, you must understand basic needs, quality worlds, total behavior, and creative systems. We have discussed all of these concepts except for the creative system, which is the topic of this chapter.

The Creative System

The creative system is one of the four components of Choice Theory. In our brains, we have a creative system that adds creativity to all of our total behaviors. This system can influence any or all of the four components of total behavior—acting, thinking, feeling, and physiology.

Creativity rarely plays a dominant role in most of the routine behaviors we choose daily. You are rarely aware of it except in certain situations. For example, we may have an unwanted thought run through our mind. Or, we may have an unwanted behavior, such as avoiding cracks as Melvin Udall did in the movie *As Good As It Gets*.

When we are creative, there is no limit as to how far our creativity can take us. Our dreams are the best example. Extremes to our creative system operating in our dreams often are called nightmares. Years ago, one of the authors, David, dreamed that he could smell colors. The smell of orange was so traumatic that he awoke from the dream. Another time, he was on a rocket ship to Mars. We all have had dreams that are beyond reality.

What our creative system does while we are awake is far more important, however. We see it clearly in the acting component of the total behavior of great athletes, dancers, surgeons, and others who perform neuromuscular feats that are creative beyond compare.

We see it clearly in the thinking component of great writers, artists, musicians, and scientists apart from the rest of us.

We see it clearly in the physiology component when people who are given up for dead create a way to recover from a severe illness—in ways that cannot be explained by medicine.

Anything that we see that is not natural was created by someone, including art, music, technology, and even philosophy (new ideas).

Every day, people are figuring out something so new and better than anything else, and they are admired for their contributions. Time passes, and other people come up with something better. On a smaller scale, most of us are frequently getting creative ideas that make improvements in our lives. For instance, we may come up with such a creative answer that we can't get over it and want to tell everyone. We saw this type of creativity at work in the movie *Castaway*.

Stranded on a deserted island after a plane crash, Tom Hanks was faced with isolation (no love and belonging). His creative system came to his aid when, in his mind, he created Wilson. Tom looked at the soccer ball initially, and you could almost see his mind working as he examined the ball. He began to build a face by drawing a pair of eyes, a nose, and a mouth. Then the name of the sports company jumped out at him as he looked at the ball: Wilson. The ball became "Wilson," Tom's "companion." He talked to Wilson on a regular basis throughout the day and night. Tom even ran his decisions by Wilson for confirmation.

This example demonstrates how the creative system can take information and reorganize it into something new to serve our purpose—in this case, as a substitute to help satisfy the need for love and belonging. If we can lend credence to the research indicating possible death from the lack of love and belonging, then Tom's creativity saved his life.

Our creativity is always available. Sometimes, it kicks in, and sometimes, it doesn't. No one can consciously call it forth. Creativity never gives up, which may or may not be a blessing. When we are unhappy and unable or unwilling to do something about it, our creativity may kick in to help us solve the problem of unhappiness.

An example of our creative system at work can be seen in the following scenario. We have just been insulted by someone and wish we had a good comeback for the cutting remark. The incident is over, and we've forgotten about it. But our creativity didn't forget. Suddenly, out of the blue, the perfect retort comes to us. As late as it comes, it still feels good. This is positive creativity.

Our creative system, however, can do us harm. An example is psychosomatic illness. The authors suspect that many of the psychosomatic illnesses observed by medical professionals in juvenile facilities are due to this problem. The juveniles' creative systems are attempting to solve unhappiness that is directly related to the juveniles' inability to meet one or more needs. Let's explore this problem by focusing on the disease of fibromyalgia.

In 1987, Dr. Frederick Wolfe, Director of the Arthritis Research Center Foundation in Wichita, Kansas brought together 20 rheumatologists from the United States and Canada. Their goal was to try to identify an unknown disorder that had continued to increase in numbers since the early 1970s. Symptoms of the disorder included persistent muscle pain throughout the body, often accompanied by severe fatigue, insomnia, diarrhea, abdominal bloating, bladder irritation, and headaches. Discussions lead to the disease being formally named fibromyalgia three years later. No pathology (abnormalities that identify a disease) has been found by the medical profession, even though the symptoms exist.

In his book *Fibromyalgia*, Glasser asks, "If fibromyalgia is not a disease, then what is it?" He continues, "While you wait for an effective medical treatment that doesn't take into account the relationship problems (that are the cause of all unhappiness; exceptions being an accident or extreme starvation), I ask you to weigh the further possibility that the pain and disability you are experiencing may be caused by something few people, doctors and patients alike, ever consider. This element, *creativity*, is very much a part of every total behavior you choose."

Why is the creative system important to staff working with juvenile offenders? When we supervise them, we often stifle their creativity. This usually occurs when we limit their opportunities to satisfy their need for freedom. Because creativity is closely tied to the need for freedom, anytime juveniles' need for freedom is thwarted, their creative system suffers as well. Juveniles *will behave*, and that behavior most likely will be "acting out." Isolation rooms in youth facilities are the recipients of these creatively deprived youth.

We will see in the following scenario how Harry's need for freedom is deprived and how his negative creativity is exhibited throughout several foster homes. His creative system is in full destructive gear, including headaching, because of the unhappiness of his life. Fortunately, Harry's path crosses the path of a loving couple who are able to connect with him. When his need for freedom is satisfied, his creativity surfaces in positive ways. We see the positive creativity of both the foster parent and the boy in full gear.

Harry is a 12-year-old juvenile whose parents were killed in an automobile accident one afternoon while he was in school. Because he had no living relatives, he was placed in foster care.

In his first foster home, Harry set fire to the pet cat and threw rocks at the neighbor's house. He was placed in a youth facility temporarily while he was undergoing counseling. This solution proved to be unsuccessful, and he was placed in a second, third, and finally a fourth foster home. Each of the experiences was a disaster. Aside from Harry's continued acting out behavior, he developed headaches that were diagnosed as migraines.

Harry arrived at his fifth foster home—the home of Fred and Martha Clemmons. With their children grown and gone, the Clemmons wanted to help some unwanted youngster. The first day, Saturday, Harry let all the air out of the tires on Fred's pickup truck. When Fred discovered the four flat tires, he knocked on Harry's bedroom door and opened it. Harry was sitting on the side of his bed, holding his head between his hands.

Mr. Clemmons:	"Good morning Harry. I wonder if you could help me."

Harry looked at the man apprehensively. Then, he rocked back and forth on the bed holding his head.

Mr. Clemmons:	"Of course, if you don't want to, that's O.K. But I have to go down to the vet and pick up a new puppy that we're getting, and I don't think I can drive and hold the pup too. Will you help me?"
Harry:	"If I could just get my head to quit hurting, maybe tomorrow."

Mr. Clemmons:	"You suppose it will hurt anymore in my old pickup than it does up here in your room? Come on, maybe Doc will let you look at some of the other animals he has boarded there. (Mr. Clemmons held out his hand.)"

Harry looked at the hand, hesitated, then reached out and took it. They went outside to the pickup truck.

Mr. Clemmons:	"Come help me get the hose hooked up to my air compressor, and you can help me fill those tires up with air."
Harry:	"Wow! I wonder how all your tires went flat at the same time?"
Mr. Clemmons:	"Probably the same way my daddy's tractor did when I was about your age. (He winked at Harry.)"
Harry:	"I've never put air in a tire before."
Mr. Clemmons:	"I'll bet you haven't. It can almost be as much fun as taking it out. (He smiled at the boy as he spoke.) Oh, by the way, how is your headache?"
Harry:	"Oh, it's better, yeah it feels a lot better. Do you want me to coil the hose up like you had?"
Mr. Clemmons:	"Why, thank you Harry, that is real helpful. While we are driving to the vet, why don't you be thinking of a name we can call this new pooch."
Harry:	"Why do you call him pooch?"
Mr. Clemmons:	"Oh, that's just the way I talk. You know, kinda like the way you young guys say dude."

Later, after they had returned with the pup, Mr. Clemmons and Harry asked Mrs. Clemmons if Pooch, the name chosen by Harry, was okay with her.

Mrs. Clemmons:	"Sounds like a real good name to me, but Mr. C., I never knew you could dream up a good name like that."

As time went by, the Clemmons and Harry became closer as they continued to connect. There was lots of love and belonging. There were rules for Harry to live by but little external control. The deadly habits were never used on the boy. There were problems, but the Clemmons and Harry always managed to work them out by discussing them and negotiating on a solution. Harry's headaches stopped, as did his acting out. He grew up in the Clemmons' home, graduated from high school, and then received his degree from the state university. He obtained a job as a landscape architect, where he put his creativity to good use.

Youth facilities and staff often miss a golden opportunity by not offering youth the freedom to be creative in a positive manner. Youth will be creative, just as they will behave, one way or another. Encouraging youth to develop hobbies is a sure way to offer them opportunities to use their creativity.

Here are three steps to help youth channel their creativity in a positive way:

Step 1: Connect with the youth. In simple terms, be friendly and care for the youth. Trust that you will see positive results with patience and time.

Step 2: Explore the youth's quality world. Ask questions and listen to youth (especially listen because when someone listens to us, it is empowering) about their areas of interest. Talk to youth about creativity, and encourage them to express their creativity in positive ways.

Step 3: Apply total behavior. Once you have information about youths' interests, what youth would like to learn and do: help them pursue those interests (acting), help them decide what and how to do it (thinking), ask how they feel about planning it (feelings), and ask how their heart is working (physiology)—just to make them aware of this component of their behavior. Remember that all counseling is teaching.

Summary

Our creative system adds creativity to all of our total behaviors and can influence our acting, thinking, feeling, and physiology. It can be helpful, such as helping us overcome unhappiness, or harmful, such as contributing to a psychosomatic illness. Helping juveniles channel their creativity in positive ways is important. Otherwise, they may use their creativity in negative ways, such as acting out behavior. Staff can help youth channel their creativity by connecting with them, exploring their quality world, and applying the information to their total behavior.

Questions

1. Our creative system can influence _____ or _____ of the four components of total behavior.

2. Our creativity is _____ available, but we cannot _____ call it forth.

3. What does connecting with youth mean?

   _____

   _____

4. What do you do with information about youths' interests?

   _____

   _____

   _____

   _____

CHAPTER 7

Introduction to Reality Therapy

Objectives

After reading this chapter, you will be able to:

- List the 13 steps of involvement
- List eight points, according to Reality Therapy, as to why people are in treatment
- Define responsibility
- Describe the importance of building a relationship with the juveniles you supervise
- Explain the importance of having good listening skills

In an earlier chapter, we mentioned that Choice Theory is the theory behind Reality Therapy. Reality Therapy is how we build a working relationship with those we are helping. It is the heart of what we do.

In this chapter, we will provide an overview of Reality Therapy and the steps of involvement. In Chapters 8, 9, 10 and 11, we will discuss the steps in more detail and how to apply them to working with juveniles.

Reality Therapy

Dr. William Glasser has had an ongoing influence on the field of corrections, both juvenile and adult. After he published *Reality Therapy*, the concepts of Reality Therapy gained the attention of people in corrections. *After all, we believe people should be held accountable, and we believe people should be responsible for their own actions.*

Unfortunately, some correctional staff misinterpreted his intention. They believed that the concepts of "reality" and "control" were things that staff could confront offenders with, and they would change. Such misinterpretation by correctional staff and others was one reason Glasser wrote *Choice Theory*. According to Glasser, *control* means that people have *control over their own lives and their choices—not that someone in an authority position controls them and their decisions.* (Glasser, *Control Theory*)

The concepts of Reality Therapy (RT) are not something that juvenile staff keep to themselves. RT can be an effective way to help juveniles learn responsible behavior. In fact, an important part of RT is teaching the steps to juveniles—so that they know what you are doing and what their involvement is, and so that they can apply the techniques themselves. Teaching helps staff develop their role as relationship builders or strength builders, not problem solvers. Therefore, RT *requires a high level of involvement—involvement of the juvenile careworker with the juvenile and total involvement of the juvenile in the process.* Now let's examine RT and how you can use it in your facility.

Eight principles explain the philosophy of Reality Therapy and why people are in treatment.

1. A belief that people choose the behavior that has led them into therapy because it is always their best effort to deal with a present, unsatisfying relationship—or worse, no relationship.
2. The task of the counselor [careworker] is to help clients [juveniles] choose new relationship-improving behaviors that are much closer to

satisfying one or more of their five basic needs than the ones currently being chosen. This means improving clients' ability to find more love and belonging, power, freedom, and fun. Survival is also a basic need, and some people come for counseling when their lives are in danger.

3. To satisfy every need, we must have good relationships with other people. This means that for many individuals, satisfying the need for love and belonging helps them satisfy the other four needs.

4. Love and belonging, like all the needs, can be satisfied only in the present. Reality Therapy focuses almost exclusively on the here and now because we can't change the past.

5. Although many of us have had unpleasant experiences in the past, we are not the victims of our past unless we presently choose to be. The solution to our problem is rarely found in explorations of the past *unless the focus is on past successes*.

6. The pain or the symptoms that clients [juveniles] choose is not important to the counseling process. We may never find out why one lonely person may choose to depress, another to obsess, a third to crazy, and a fourth to drink. In fact, if we focus on the symptom, we enable the client [juvenile] to avoid the real problem, which is improving present relationships.

7. The continuing goal of Reality Therapy is for the counselor [careworker] to connect with the client [juvenile]. By experiencing this satisfying relationship, clients [juveniles] can learn a lot about how to improve the troubled relationship that brought them into counseling.

8. To understand why the seven principles just mentioned are integral to practicing Reality Therapy, the counselor [careworker] and client [juvenile] should read the 1998 book, *Choice Theory: A New Psychology of Personal Freedom*, and the 1999 book, *The Language of Choice Theory*. If clients [juveniles] can't or won't read these books, the therapist [careworker] can teach them the Choice Theory they need to know as the counseling proceeds.

Robert E. Wubbolding, Ph.D., Center for Reality Therapy/Midwest, defines Realty Therapy as: "... a method of helping people take better control of their lives. It helps people to identify and to clarify what they want and what they need and then to evaluate whether they can realistically attain what they want. It helps them to examine their own behaviors and to evaluate them with clear criteria. This is followed by positive planning designed to help control their own lives as well as fulfill their realistic wants and their needs. The result is added strength, more self-confidence, better human relations, and a personal plan for a more effective life. It, thus, provides people with a self-help tool to use daily to cope with adversity, to grow personally, and to get more effective control of their lives.

"Reality Therapy is based on several principles, such as:

"People are responsible for their own behavior—not society, not heredity, not past history;

"People can change and live more effective lives;

"People behave for a purpose—to mold their environment as a sculptor molds clay, to match their own inner pictures of what they want.

The intended results described are achievable through continuous effort and hard work."

Glasser sums up the principles of RT by saying:

"Our basic job . . . is to become involved with the (juvenile) and then persuade him to face reality. When confronted with reality, it is his choice as to whether he will take the responsible path." (Glasser, *Reality Therapy*)

Glasser defines responsibility as "the ability to satisfy one's needs without interfering with the ability of others to satisfy their needs." He refers to those who act contrary to this definition as irresponsible. Once again, you can help juveniles learn responsible behaviors by using the principles of RT and teaching them Choice Theory.

In previous chapters, we discussed that our basic needs, like a motor in a car, provide the power that drives us. The five basic needs are: the need to survive and reproduce, the need to belong and be loved, the need for power, the need for freedom, and the need for fun. We all have these needs, but we vary in our ability to fulfill them. In addition, the intensity of the needs may vary from person to person. We can fulfill these needs successfully by becoming involved with other people. At all times, we must have at least one person in our life who genuinely cares about us and whom we genuinely care about. This person, who must be in touch with reality and able to fulfill his or her own needs, helps us to satisfy our need for belonging. Without this person or other people in our lives, we may try unrealistic ways to fulfill our need to belong and be loved. We may begin to choose problem behaviors ranging from mild anxiety to complete denial of reality.

As we learned in the Basic Needs chapter, we sometimes can satisfy our need for power, fun and freedom by ourselves. But we need another person to help us satisfy our need to belong and be loved.

All the juveniles in our care, custody and control have not been able to fulfill their needs in a lawful and/or socially acceptable manner. This inability manifests itself in delinquent or irresponsible behavior, which is the juveniles' vain attempt to reach personal fulfillment. You can make a connection with the youth in your care and help them meet their needs in a law-abiding way—especially their need for love and belong. The key to making the connection is involvement.

Alex Bassen, an associate of Dr. Glasser, has identified 13 steps of involvement. They are:

1. Be **warm-friendly**.

2. **Reveal yourself** (which we call **self-disclosure**—share your interests with the juvenile).

3. Use pronouns **I** and **me**.

4. Discuss the **here** and **now**.

5. **Discuss behavior**, not feelings.

6. Ask **what**, **not why**.

7. **Have juveniles evaluate** their own behavior.

8. Help juveniles work out a **plan**.

9. Make a **contract**.

10. **Accept no excuses**.

11. Work in **groups**.

12. **P-A-R-T: praise, approve, reward, touch**.

13. **DON'T GIVE UP!!!**

We believe that these steps provide a good "roadmap" for how to practice Reality Therapy. We will be discussing them in detail in the following chapters.

In Chapter 8, *Establishing a Working Relationship* (basically making friends with the juveniles), we will discuss:

- Step 1: Be warm-friendly.
- Step 2: Reveal yourself.
- Step 3: Use pronouns I and me.

In Chapter 9, *Planning for Behavioral Change*, we will discuss:

- Step 7: Have juveniles evaluate their own behavior.
- Step 8: Help juveniles work out a plan.
- Step 9: Make a contract.

In Chapter 10, *Working with Groups*, we will discuss:

- Step 11: Work in groups.

In Chapter 11, *Don't Give Up*, we will discuss:

- Step 12: P-A-R-T: praise, approve, reward, touch.
- Step 13: Don't give up.

In the remainder of this chapter, we will discuss the four steps that we believe are not only unique to RT but also which provide a foundation for it.

- Step 4: Discuss the here and now.
- Step 5: Discuss behavior, not feelings.
- Step 6: Ask what, not why.
- Step 10: Accept no excuses.

Steps 4, 5, and 6 of Involvement

The effectiveness of RT rests upon your discussions with the juvenile. Steps 4-6 provide direction for having discussions with juveniles. The steps are:

4. Discuss the **here** and **now**.
5. **Discuss behavior**, not feelings.
6. Ask **what, not why**.

According to RT, you should *not* discuss:

- **Their past history.** Juveniles break the law and are irresponsible because they are unhappy. Juveniles are unhappy because a relationship is not satisfying or is not present. The juveniles' past history should not play a role in their treatment because it has no bearing upon the present reality and cannot help them learn responsible behaviors. If someone stole your little red wagon when you were three, what can you do to change that now?

- **Unhappiness as the problem.** Choice Theory believes that there is one problem in the world, unhappiness. The cause of the unhappiness is a relationship that is not satisfying to the juvenile or a lack of a relationship. Love and belonging are the hardest of the basic needs for us to meet because we need another person to meet them. Therefore, during discussions with juveniles, you should discuss their unhappiness and help them explore ways of connecting with others and satisfying their need to belong and be loved.

Glasser says, "I know several things about any client, juvenile or adult, before I begin counseling. One, I know the person is unhappy, and it is because of a relationship. I also know that the person is going to want to talk about the past to avoid the relationship problem that is the cause of the unhappiness. I also know the person will want to talk about the symptoms for the same reason, and it also casts them into the victim's role: 'It *happened* to me, therefore I am not responsible for my behavior.'" (Glasser, *Reality Therapy*) You can see from these statements that external control thinking is of no benefit to the helping process.

RT says that you *should talk* with juveniles about their:

- **Present life and relate it, when possible, to the juveniles' behavior.** You should try to make juveniles aware that there is life beyond their difficulties, and that problems can be solved and life started anew.
- **Interests, opinions, hopes, fears, and values (their ideas of right and wrong).** This practice shows juveniles that you are interested in them as persons with potential, not just problems.

Focusing your conversations on these areas serves two purposes; it:

- **Helps juveniles realize that they can have a responsible attitude toward most facets of life.** They learn by testing your opinions on various subjects. For example, they may ask, "Do you get up on time?" or "How often do you get your car repaired?" Such questions allow them to explore your responsible behaviors and see that responsible behavior is, indeed, a daily fact of life for many people.

- **Increases the juveniles' self-worth.** This situation occurs when juveniles "check out" their beliefs and values with you, a trustworthy and responsible person.

To keep juveniles focused on the present, Glasser recommends that you and the juvenile always search for the answer to "What is wrong?"—rather than "Why is it wrong?" He points out that all the reasons in the world for why an alcoholic drinks will not make him stop. Similarly, we can apply this logic to delinquent juveniles. Youth often do not know why they did something. Moreover, knowing why they broke the law will not deter their delinquent behavior. Asking "What did you hope to accomplish" is better than asking "Why?" Specifically, ask "What is your goal?" and "How did this help you accomplish your goal?"

Step 10, "Accept no excuses," is critical to the success of Reality Therapy. If juveniles fail to do what they said they would do, you should not accept any excuses for the failure. If all behavior is purposeful, then the juveniles have chosen to behave in this manner. Likewise, you should not lecture the juveniles. Instead, help them see where they made the decision to do what they chose to do rather than do what was expected. The following example illustrates this point.

Gregory was late for his group therapy appointment. He has been late the last two times as well, and always by 15 minutes.

Group: "Hey, how come Gregory always gets to come late?"
Gregory: "The bus was late."

This kind of diatribe took up another ten minutes of the group's time. At the end of the hour, I asked Gregory to remain so that we could have a little individual discussion.

Gregory:	"Hey man, what did I do? How come I have to stay over and none of the others do?"
David:	"Well man, I thought maybe you and I could talk about your responsibility to make group without the possibility of embarrassing you in front of the group. Like, if you have a bathroom problem or have to stay after school for some reason or something else that you would prefer the group not hear. Is that O.K.?"
Gregory:	"Hell no, it's none of that stuff, I told you IT'S THE BUS. IT'S ALWAYS LATE."
David:	"O.K. O.K. That should be easy enough to solve. What cha goin' to do about it?"
Gregory:	"What do you mean? I can't drive the damn thing. It's always late."
David:	"I will be willing to help you make the meetings on time, so let's look at some things. What time do you get out of your last class before you have to catch the bus?"
Gregory:	"I don't remember."
David:	"When we set up the time for the group meeting, as I remember it, you have social studies, and the class ends at 3:15. Does that sound right with you, or do we need to call the school office?"
Gregory:	"No, I remember now, it's 3:15."

Notice that the questions to Gregory are ones designed to help him think.

David:	"And what time does the bus you are suppose to catch stop at the school?"
Gregory:	"I'm not sure, maybe four."
David:	"As I remember it, there is one at 3:30, one at 3:45, and the one you have been catching, which is 4:00. Do we need to call the office to verify those bus times?"

Gregory:	"Now that you mention it, those are the bus times."
David:	"How long does it take to get from school to group? Fifteen minutes, isn't it?"
Gregory:	"Yeah, I think so."
David:	"And group starts at 4:00, right? (Gregory nodded.) So, let's check your math. You do pretty well in there because the last time I talked with your teacher, you were making a B. That's great. So, if it takes 15 minutes to get here, which bus do you need to catch in order to make it on time?"
Gregory:	"(Resignedly.) The 3:45 bus."
David:	"Will you do that from now on, or even the 3:30 bus?"
Gregory:	"Yes, I will."
David:	"And if you don't, what do you think should be the consequences?"
Gregory:	"I'll make it. I'll make it."
David:	"O.K. Sounds good. Tell me Gregory, before we leave, do you want to see me alone in addition to meeting with the group?"
Gregory:	"Hell no, why would you ask me such a dumb question?"
David:	"O.K. Just group then. But I thought maybe by being late, you were giving me the message you needed some individual attention. If that is the case, I suppose you will continue to be late. Is that a fair assumption?"
Gregory:	"(Grinning at me.) I won't be late again. I don't want to have to come in here like this again."

We shook hands, and I said, "Looks like we have a contract. Deal!"

Summary

Reality Therapy is an effective way to help juveniles learn responsible behavior. According to William Glasser, at the heart of juveniles' problems is an unsatisfying relationship or lack of a relationship. By connecting with juveniles, you can help them learn to have a positive relationship and satisfy their needs in law-abiding ways. Connecting with juveniles requires intense involvement. When you're talking with juveniles, you should discuss the present and their current behaviors. If juveniles fail to keep their word, you should help them see where they made the decision to choose to do the opposite of what they committed to do.

Questions

1. According to William Glasser, what does having control mean?

   _____

   _____

2. An important part of Reality Therapy is _____ the steps to juveniles.

3. Good _____ are the key to healthy lives.

4. Define the term responsibility.

   _____

   _____

5. What should you talk to juveniles about?

   _____

   _____

6. True/False. If juveniles fail, you should accept the failure as part of the overall plan and try again.

7. True/False. To focus on the present, you and the juvenile should search for the answer to "Why is it wrong?"

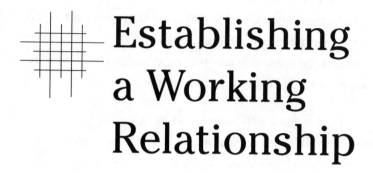

CHAPTER 8

Establishing a Working Relationship

Objectives

After reading this chapter, you will be able to:

- List the first three steps of involvement
- Discuss a continuum of social relationships
- List the seven deadly habits that destroy relationships
- Identify three things you must have in building a relationship
- Identify five faults of listening
- Identify six things you must do to improve your listening skills

In this chapter, we will discuss why developing a relationship with juveniles is important for staff and why they often resist doing so. We will look at a continuum of social relationships that moves from hostile to friendly. We also will explore the importance of listening, the common listening faults that we have, and how to overcome them.

Steps 1, 2, and 3 of Involvement

The first three steps of involvement help you build a relationship with a juvenile. They are:

- **Be warm-friendly.**
- **Reveal yourself or self-disclose—share your interests.**
- **Use pronouns I and me .**

Becoming involved with juveniles requires that you build a firm, emotional relationship with them—to become friends with juveniles.

We find that most staff have difficulty accepting the idea that they should be friends with the juveniles. Staff often resist this concept. They have been cautioned to avoid losing their objectivity and becoming "overly" involved with juveniles. Thus, staff usually are concerned about "being taken advantage of," "manipulated," or "conned." Let's put the idea of being a friend, building a relationship, into a more acceptable framework. Below is a continuum of social relationships among human groups:

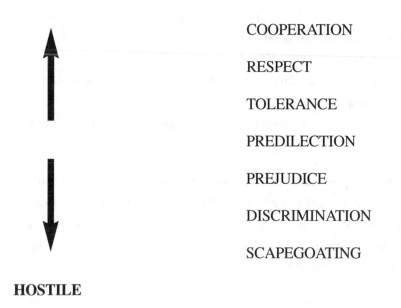

FRIENDLY

COOPERATION

RESPECT

TOLERANCE

PREDILECTION

PREJUDICE

DISCRIMINATION

SCAPEGOATING

HOSTILE

We have seen some juvenile and adult facilities where the prevailing attitudes and relationships between the workers and the residents are based on:

- **Prejudice**—forming an unfavorable opinion or feeling beforehand or without knowledge
- **Discrimination**—having an opinion about a person based on the group, class or category to which the person belongs rather than on individual merit
- **Scapegoating**—assigning blame or failure to someone

These negative beliefs are very close to the seven deadly habits of criticizing, blaming, complaining, nagging, threatening, punishing and bribing. These beliefs will put an end to any relationship. In fact, they usually prevent a relationship from building. Our experience has shown us that treatment does not take place in such an environment and that positive change on the part of the offenders does not occur.

When we talk about "making friends" or "becoming friends" with juveniles, we are talking about moving up the continuum of social relationships—not crossing boundaries into an inappropriate relationship or being manipulated. If you can't be "friends," you at least can have:

- **Predilection**— a preexisiting tendency to think favorably of someone
- **Tolerance**—a fair and objective attitude toward those whose opinions, practices, race, religion, nationality, and so forth differ from your own

When building a relationship with juveniles, you must be prepared to handle resistance from them. This resistance is the juveniles' way of testing your sincerity. The key to involvement is neither to give up nor to push too hard.

To develop a relationship with juveniles, you first must have:

- **Respect**—esteem for or a sense of the worth or excellence of a person
- **A sense of cooperation**—an act or instance of working or acting together for a common purpose or benefit

The next step in developing a relationship with juveniles is to establish trust with them. Relationships are built on a foundation of trust. Trust is earned—not just given because someone has a title or a position. To earn juveniles trust, you must be open and honest, and share your interests. You must be clear about what you can and cannot do. You also must be ethical or fair in your use of power and authority. You must not use your position for personal gain, and you must not use your power inappropriately.

For example:

- **Be honest and open about the use of your authority.** Never make a recommendation or report about a juvenile without sharing the information with the juvenile. If you are going to make a recommendation that will restrict his or her freedom, tell the juvenile you are doing so. Be honest in what you do.
- **Do not use threats, bluffing, or any behavior that might cloud rather than clarify your authority.**
- **Exercise your authority with empathic understanding of the juvenile's needs as a person—a person always worthy of your interest, respect and affection.** This practice makes your role reconstructive rather than retributive, helping rather than punishing, a friend rather than an enemy.

To earn juveniles trust, you also must listen to them. In our discussions with juveniles, we are often more concerned with what we will say next than we are in listening and observing. Psychologist Carl Rogers states that the "biggest barrier to effective communication is our inability to listen." Listening is not only an important skill to use with juveniles but also staff members and other people in our lives. We are not born with the ability to listen effectively. We learn how to listen and must continually work on developing the skill.

To listen effectively, you must avoid being preoccupied. If you cannot be fully focused on the conversation you are having with juveniles, they will know it. You will grow further apart instead of connecting and getting closer. We hear with our ears, but we listen with our eyes, mind, heart, skin and guts as well. Listening involves hearing the way things are being said, and the tone, expressions and gestures being used. It also involves hearing what is not being said, what is only hinted at, what is perhaps being held back, and what lies beneath or beyond the surface.

Our goal is to listen with understanding. Here is a simple test to show you how well you are listening. State in your own words what a juvenile has just said and ask whether you have heard him or her correctly. If the juvenile says yes, then you probably have truly listened to and understood the juvenile.

In addition to helping us establish trust with juveniles, listening also helps us satisfy juveniles' need for power. Choice Theory says that when we listen to another person, we are helping the person satisfy his or her need for power.

Dr. Ralph Nichols, former head of the Rhetoric Department at the University of Minnesota, identified ten faults with listening.

1. Deciding, even before the speaker starts, that the subject will be uninteresting and unimportant
2. Criticizing the speaker's delivery, clothes, haircut, or anything else
3. Becoming too involved in—and emotional—when questioning or opposing an idea
4. Listening only for facts and skipping the details
5. Trying to make an outline of everything
6. Faking attention and withdrawing or daydreaming
7. Tolerating or creating distractions
8. Ignoring difficult material

9. Over-reacting to certain words and phrases
10. Mentally lining up arguments to counter what is said

To improve your listening skills, you must:

- Listen for the total message—verbal and nonverbal
- Check your body and head posture—make sure that you are listening with your body as well as your ears; make sure that you are facing the juvenile, making appropriate eye contact (taking cultural practices into consideration), and leaning forward slightly (to show interest)
- Listen for meaning in content and feelings that are expressed
- Listen with understanding of where the other person is
- Ask yourself:
     What is the juvenile telling me?
     What does it mean to them?
- Check out what you heard

Let's see how David uses his listening and observation skills in working with Donnie. Often, when we're using Choice Theory and Reality Therapy, we need more information. More information can be the difference between quality counseling and good counseling, or good counseling and bad counseling. The following scenario is an example of what can happen when the counselor gets more information.

Donnie is a 13-year-old on probation violation. He has no father or mother and has lived in welfare foster homes since he was nine. Donnie was adjudicated delinquent after breaking into three homes and spray-painting the walls. He also broke two television sets and stole $27.00 in bills and coins off the top of a bedroom dresser. At his dispositional hearing, he was placed on probation. Barbara was assigned as his probation officer.

Donnie had been on probation for three weeks and was referred again when he stole a bicycle. He was placed in detention pending another hearing on violating his probation.

As Director of Court Services, I frequently visited the detention facility to observe the population rate and how the facility was functioning. During one of my visits, I heard shouting in the visiting room. I opened the door and encountered a very angry probation officer wagging her finger in the face of a very bewildered young man.

Barbara: "I'm having some difficulty with Donnie. He refuses to talk to me. I guess I got a little loud."

I smiled at Barbara and said hello to Donnie.

David: "Oh, you might have awakened some of the animals that were hibernating in the Tulsa Zoo, but that's all right, they will just get an early start this year, I think." (Notice that I do not use external control or any of the deadly habits with Barbara.)

Barbara: "Can I talk to you outside?"

David: "Sure."

We stepped outside the room, and Barbara vented her frustration.

Barbara: "I can't stand this kid, I'm sorry. He will not talk to me, and I'm so frustrated I don't know what to do. Do you think Bob would reassign him to another officer?"

Bob was the probation supervisor, and one of his duties was to assign the juveniles just adjudicated delinquent to a probation officer.

Barbara: "I can work with most kids, even the really tough street walkers and dope addicts we get. But how can you be expected to work with a kid who won't even answer you? You saw him. When you said good morning to him, he just stared at you. That's what he does to me all the time. I tell you David, I've had it."

David: "O.K. O.K. Barbara. You're a good probation counselor and help a lot of kids. You go on back to the probation offices and let me talk with, or rather, maybe I should say at him. Then, I'll come back over, and we'll see what Bob, you and I can do. O.K.?"

Barbara: "Oh thank you. It's like talking to a wall. The arresting officers told me I wouldn't be able to get anything out of him. When I told them 'that'll be the day,' I didn't know what I was in for. He hasn't said three sentences to me since I became his probation officer. Good luck in your efforts."

I went back into the visiting room where Donnie sat quietly and looked up at me as I entered. I spoke to him again and smiled at him. I offered my hand, and he limply took it. I did all the shaking. He said nothing.

David: "Donnie, my name's David. Can I sit down and talk with you for a couple of minutes?"

The young man just looked at me and said nothing. Then, he turned his head and looked at the wall.

David: "Look, you don't have to talk to me if you don't want to. Would you rather not?"

Donnie continued looking at the wall and then back at me.

Reality Therapy and Choice Theory

David: "Now look, if you don't want to talk with me just nod your head. Thank you. Since you haven't nodded your head, I guess it is all right. If it is, don't move."

"Donnie just stared at me and did and said nothing. I began to appreciate Barbara's frustration.

David: "Since you are having trouble in the foster home, do you think you would like to live at Lakeside?"

Lakeside is a residential treatment center that is coed. Several of us had helped develop the facility from just a warehouse for kids to a fine treatment facility for the nonviolent youngsters. The more violent youth that could not be helped on probation were transferred to the state reformatory.

Donnie just stared at me some more. I knew that if there was an event for staring in the Olympics, Donnie could go for the gold.

David: "Donnie, I won't bug you much longer, but just answer me one question, and I'll get out of your hair. If you had a magic wand, what would you wish for right now?"

I sat back and stared at Donnie. His eyes never wavered, they just kept staring. I thought, 'I wonder if I can keep mine open before having to blink, longer than he can?' Several seconds went by.

Donnie: "I would go fishing at my grandma's."

I was hoping my mouth hadn't dropped open. I felt like it had. What in the world was going on with this kid? While I was contemplating the events, Donnie continued to talk.

Donnie: "I know some kids at Lakeside. I would like that."

Now I was the one tongue-tied. What was with this kid? I tried an experiment.

David: "Donnie, what kind of bait do you use when you fish with
           your grandma?"

I waited patiently while Donnie stared at me some more. After awhile, he continued.

Donnie: "Usually, grandma would dig some worms, but sometimes we
           caught grasshoppers."
David: "Did you eat the fish you caught?"

This time, I glanced at my watch and waited. In twenty seconds, Donnie answered me.

Donnie: "Yeah, grandma would clean them and fry them up. They
           were real good."
David: "How has school been for you Donnie?"

It took exactly twenty seconds again.

Donnie: "I'm two grades back, the teachers get real mad at me 'cause I
           don't learn too well."
David: "Have you ever had special tutors? Do you know what a tutor
           is?"

Two questions, but it still took twenty seconds. This kid just took longer to process the information that was being put to him. No wonder he was having so many people problems.

Donnie:	(20 seconds) "I know what they are, but they always got mad at me."
David:	"Donnie, when you took that bicycle, what was it that you really wanted?"
Donnie:	(20 seconds) "I just wanted to get something of my own. I don't ever get to do things like other kids, so I make up things to do."
David:	"Is taking other peoples things, you know, stealing, against the law?"
Donnie:	(20 seconds) "I know, but nobody has ever cared much about me taking stuff before."
David:	"Donnie, who do you think cares the most about you in this world?"

This time, he looked away and then stared at the floor. Twenty seconds went by, and another twenty. Finally, he looked at me and there were tears in his eyes. Then, he began to talk.

Donnie:	"When I was a little boy, I remember my mother used to hold me real close. Then, one day when we were driving down the highway, a big old semi hit our car, and my mama was killed. I was in the hospital for a long time they tell me. When I got out, they put me in a foster home because my grandmother had died of a heart attack when she learned my mama was killed. So, nobody really cares for me, but that's all right. I don't need nobody anyway."

I handed him a couple of tissues and continued.

David:	"Donnie, you know that you take a little longer to answer people's questions than a lot of kids do, don't you?"
Donnie:	(20 seconds) "Yes, but nobody ever lets me talk. You're the first person since my Granny who has let me talk."

David: "I'll make a deal with you Donnie. I'll explain to Mrs. Barbara what the deal is. That you give things a little more thought than some kids do, and for her to just wait for you. Then you can talk with her too. O.K.?"

Donnie grinned, but it took twenty seconds.

Donnie: "Yeah, I can do that."
David: "O.K. I'll see you later, how about five?"

Donnie gave me five, but it took twenty to do it. Later, I talked with Barbara, and she was delighted to find out about the processing delay. We later learned that Donnie had sustained some brain injury in the auto accident that had killed his mother. Donnie lived at Lakeside for three years, caught up in his school-work with special education, and later entered high school. Further information made a difference for Donnie, his probation officer, and society too.

Developing a relationship with a juvenile will become easier once you have acquired the qualities or traits you need to teach Choice Theory. These traits include:

- Being a responsible person—sensitive
- Being able to fulfill your own needs and being willing to discuss some of your own struggles so that the juvenile can see that acting responsibly is possible, though difficult
- Possessing the strength to become involved, to withstand criticism or requests for sympathy, and to have your values tested by the juvenile. You must be strong enough to point out reality to the juvenile no matter how hard he or she resists it. The juvenile may even insist you condone his or her irresponsible behavior.
- Investing a great deal of your time, energy and concern into the process
- Showing that you care about what the juvenile does and believing that his or her values are important

- Allowing the juvenile to go through emotional pain if it will help him or her learn about responsibility—"letting go"
- Accepting the juvenile as he or she is. You must not be "turned off" or frightened by the juvenile's behavior, whether he or she curses or inflicts wounds upon himself or herself (e.g., making marks with a pen or cuts with a sharp object)

Developing involvement or building a relationship with a juvenile may take anywhere from one meeting to several months, depending on your skill and the resistance of the juvenile. Once involvement occurs and throughout the process, you must insist that the juvenile confront the reality of his behavior. You must not accept any excuses for irresponsible behavior.

The following scenario of Leroy will clarify this issue. Leroy is a 16-year-old male referred to David for sexually molesting a nine-year-old girl. Leroy was assigned to another probation officer for three weeks. The officer accepted a position in another city, and the case was transferred to me. My first visit was to Leroy's school. The school always provided an office for me to meet with any probationers I had who attended their school.

First Meeting

Leroy shuffled through the door and without looking at me, he took a seat against the wall as far from the chair where I sat as he could.

David: "Hi Leroy, my name is David, and I'm your new probation officer." I didn't wait for an answer and continued talking to him.
"I hope we can be friendly with each other, and to do that we will be talking together for some time. So, since I don't have my hearing aide on, I'll just move closer so I can hear any thing you might decide to say. Is that O.K. with you?"

My chair had rollers on it, so not waiting for an answer, I rolled my chair closer to his. Leroy stared at me in disbelief.

Leroy:	"You ain't for real man, are you?"
David:	"Wadda ya mean?" I asked innocently.
Leroy:	"You go rollin' chairs around like you wasn't no probation cop. What you dealin' out to me?"
David:	"Look, I'm going to be honest with you Leroy. My title is probation officer, O.K.? When I get my check at the end of the month, it says probation officer. But that doesn't mean I don't care about the guys and gals that are on my caseload. You and I don't know each other, and I would like to know you better. Is there anything wrong with that?"
Leroy:	Leroy stared at me as he spoke, "Yeah! I DON'T want to know you at all, not better, not at all."

Now is the challenge. Both Leroy and I are in an externally controlled system, that is, the juvenile court, and I must first acknowledge to Leroy this real information. Then, I must attempt to form a relationship with him using as little external control as I possibly can. Where I can't, I will point out that the law, the judge, the court, and the system are putting external control on him. I also will describe how he can live a better life when he advances to the point where he is no longer subject to the external control.

David:	"Well, ole buddy," I said. "WE don't have a choice." I emphasized we.
Leroy:	He sat up straight. "What does that mean?"
David:	"It means, my friend, that you and I are like the Lone Ranger and Tonto. The juvenile judge puts his name on a piece of paper that says you and I will see each other EVERY WEEK! Now, do you want to be the Lone Ranger, or do you want to be Tonto?"

Leroy:	"My God, I've inherited a nut." He sat and shook his head.
David:	"Look Leroy, I'm not such a bad guy. In fact, most of the kids like me pretty well. Why do you suppose that is?"
Leroy:	"You're entertaining. You are a real joke, man." Leroy spat out the words.
David:	"Well, I'll tell you why they like me and why you will eventually think I'm an O.K. guy. I will shoot straight with you, and I won't lie or harass you. I WILL insist on seeing you every week, because my boss, the judge, the court, the law, says I will. So, hey let's make the best of it. What have you got to lose? Might keep you out of jail."
Leroy:	"What if it does? What do you mean when you say you won't harass me? What does that mean?"
David:	"It means, all I want to do is spend a little time each week, and the two of us just talk. You probably haven't had an adult who just wanted to talk with you ever. Isn't that true?"
Leroy:	"Maybe. What will we talk about? Me listen, and you preach?"
David:	"No, no. We'll just talk about things that might be what you want to do with your life. I don't know. What things would you like to talk about?"
Leroy:	"I want to talk about pot. I know where you and I can get a load of the stuff and sell it off and make a bundle. What say?" He studied me carefully.
David:	"I don't guess you are going to be the Lone Ranger OR Tonto. You want for you and me to be the cattle rustlers. I'm afraid that dog won't hunt, if you get my drift. Do you?" Now I studied him carefully.
Leroy:	He grinned and said, "I knew you were straight the moment I set eyes on you man. I never knowed a straight dude that I could trust, and you ain't gonna be any different."
David:	"Well," I said, "Our time is about up. I need to get on to my next interview, and you need to get back into class. First, let

me ask you something, and you don't have to answer now. But I want an answer next week when we talk again. What would it look like to you, if you could trust me? I kinda like to shake hands with the guys I talk with, O.K.?"

Leroy: Leroy refused to shake hands and shuffled on back to his next class.

Second Meeting

Leroy: Leroy shuffled into the room and immediately said, "I don't feel no good today, so I ain't talkin to you, and that's the truth."

David: "That's fine Leroy, I'm sorry to hear you don't feel well. Have you been to the nurse's office?" He just stared straight ahead, so I continued. "Well, I'm concerned about your health, so I'm going to have us do one of two things, and you can choose which one. One, we'll go to the nurse's office, or if you don't feel like doing that, I will call her to come down here. Which will it be?"

Leroy: "I'm feelin some better," he sighed, "I may not need to see her at all."

David: "Well, that's good news Leroy. Now, I asked you a question just before we broke up our meeting last week."
I didn't wait to ask him if he remembered, I just continued on. "What would it look like if you did trust me?"

Leroy: "That is the dumbest question I ever did hear in my whole life."

David: "What is your whole life? Fourteen years or what?"

Leroy: "Man I'm almost seventeen. Not no fourteen."

David: "O.K. Sounds like you are working on becoming a man. When do you think you will make it?"

Leroy:	Leroy glared at me. "I'm practically on my own now, if it weren't for school, and I'll quit before long anyway."
David:	"If you quit school, where will the judge send you?"
Leroy:	"I don't know. He won't know. If you want me to trust you, then you can't tell him."
David:	"Well, Leroy, I read the transcript of your hearing, and the judge set down some pretty strict rules with the consequences being that you will lose your freedom. Now, I gotta ask. Is that something you want to happen? Lose your freedom?"
Leroy:	"It don't matter. You gonna do what you want anyway."
David:	"Leroy, what do you want to happen that isn't against the rules?"
Leroy:	"I want off probation man. But I suppose that is against the rules?"
David:	"What do you have to do if you want off probation?"

Leroy just stared at me.

David:	"Come on. There are several, but let's just look at one. What is one thing you have to do to get off probation?"
Leroy:	"I don't know."
David:	I produced a list of his probation rules set down by the court. "Here is the first one. Do you want to read it or have me read it? It's your choice."
Leroy:	"You're the smart one, so read it."
David:	"Juvenile will abstain from further delinquent behavior. Do you know what abstain means?"
Leroy:	"Look, I'm not no retard, of course I know what it means."
David:	"Help me to understand. What do you think it means?"
Leroy:	"It means don't do that stuff no more. There, you happy?"
David:	"Are you going to do that stuff anymore?"
Leroy:	"No man. I'm cool."

David: "O.K. We have that covered, now let's take one more. Here is the next one. Remain in high school, and do passing work."

Leroy: "Is that on that paper?"

David: I showed Leroy where it was typed on the paper. "The office tells me you are making Ds in all your courses except math and social studies. You have a C in math and an F in social studies."

Leroy: "Hey man, you checkin' on me?"

David: "Yes, I am, and I will continue until we can become friends and discuss all this openly and honestly. However, I won't criticize or blame you. I'm trying to help you so you can get off probation. Is that cool with you?"

Leroy: "Yeah, yeah, but I hate social studies."

David: "That's O.K. Let's talk about math. Man, that C looks pretty good along side of all those other grades. You must like math, is that correct?"

Leroy: "Yeah but especially the teacher. He is real cool."

David: "What is cool about him?"

Leroy: "He let's us have fun in class. No other class in school lets us have fun."

David: "I know a way you can have a tiny bit of fun in all your classes."

Leroy: "Now how in the hell am I suppose to have fun in English? Answer me that smart ass."

Often, delinquent youngsters will use this kind of language, or worse, to detour any discussion of their choosing their "bad" behavior, or being responsible for it. I'm not going to get sucked into an argument or criticizing him on etiquette. No kid ever stopped his or her delinquent behavior because he or she gave up using four letter words.

David: "Can you read, or do you have difficulty?"

Leroy:	"Yeah, I can read O.K. if I want. What does that have to do with anything?"
David:	"I'll tell you. Since you can read, English is a problem because you don't enjoy it, is that correct?" He nodded, and I continued. "If you are willing to give it a shot, I will help you have a little bit of fun in that class."
Leroy:	"I ask you again, how?"
David:	"Well, tell me what your next assignment is and when it is due."
Leroy:	He fumbled with his backpack and finally produced a stack of English papers and a textbook. "Here it is. We are suppose to read the first two chapters that describe a book named *The Source*, by a guy named Mitchner. It is probably the dryest crap in the world."
David:	"O.K. Open it, and let's look at the first chapter. What does it say the book is about?"
Leroy:	"It's about diggin' up old bones and stuff ancient people had before they were killed or died or something."
David:	"Do you like your nanny, your grandmother?"
Leroy:	"What in the hell does that have to do with English? You are one weird dude."
David:	"Come on. Do you like your nanny?"
Leroy:	"Yes, of course I do. She practically raised me. Why?"
David:	"Where was she born?"
Leroy:	Leroy looked at me, then shook his head. "I don't know, Alabama I think. Why?"
David:	"Where was her grandmother born?"
Leroy:	"How would I know? I think she said something about her nanny and grandfather being slaves, yeah, I remember she said that."
David:	"Would you like to know where they were born, and then suppose you could know where their grandparents were born,

	and what kind of things they did in their lives, would you be interested? In other words, where your roots came from?"
Leroy:	"Not particularly. Where did yours come from?"
David:	"Oh my, my background is really varied. Some Irish, some English, some German, some Norwegian, some Dutch, and I don't know what else. But I think it is interesting to find out how our ancestors lived, and what kind of houses they had, and what they ate. What do you think?"
Leroy:	"Readin' *The Source* isn't going to tell me nothin' about my roots. Is it?"

This response is a good sign. Leroy is actually carrying on a conversation with me and is showing some interest in the subject. I'll just keep talking with him to make the connection we need to help him self-evaluate. Without self-evaluation, there will not be any positive change over and above conformity. Unfortunately, in schools and in corrections, we most often opt for conformity rather than change toward a quality life.

David:	"If you give this book a chance, you may discover other books that deal with your ancestors' birthplace and lifestyle. Believe me, if you discover that, you will understand what I meant when I said you could have fun in your other classes."
Leroy:	"O.K. I'll give it a shot. What do you want me to do?"
David:	"Try reading a couple of pages and see how it feels. You may be surprised. If you feel no different than you did before you read them, will you have lost anything other than a few minutes?"
Leroy:	"I just don't have the time to read even two pages."
David:	"Tell you what. We've still got a few minutes before our time is up this week. Suppose I read a couple of pages with you. Do you mind?"
David:	Leroy agreed, and after we took turns reading aloud, I asked him, "What do you remember about what we read?"

Leroy:	"I learned what a tell is."
David:	"Tell me, ha, ha. What is a tell as you remember it?"
Leroy:	"A tell is what those archeologist call the place that they are digging and uncovering old stuff."
David:	"Absolutely. Great! How does that feel?"
Leroy:	"It feels good, but why would that feel good?"
David:	Now is my opportunity to teach a little Choice Theory to Leroy. "When you learn something new, our genes reward us with the good feeling of fun. Would you like to feel that fun feeling some more?"
Leroy:	"Yeah, what do I have to do?"
David:	"You don't have to do anything, but if you choose to, you can read some more and learn some more stuff that makes you feel good. Hey, it even works in social studies."
Leroy:	"You're different from the other probation officers. How come?"
David:	"I don't know who the other officers were. What do you think is the difference?"
Leroy:	Leroy thought for several seconds before he said anything. Then he looked me in the eye. "You listen to what I have to say, and ask me what I think about things."

Listening to another person is very empowering. With these youngsters, satisfying their power needs acceptably is a difficult thing to do. Most of them have not learned how to satisfy their needs other than by delinquent behavior.

I saw Leroy once and sometimes twice a week for the next three months. With the help of his teachers, Leroy improved his school performance and passed his junior year. I saw him monthly for another five months, and he was released from probation in the middle of his senior year.

I received an invitation to attend his high school graduation, which I did. Two years later, I received a letter from him. He was stationed in Germany. He wrote about what he was doing and ended by writing that he had received two promotions and was planning on making the army his career. He signed it, "Your Friend."

The next scenario of Jesse demonstrates that friendship can develop early in a juvenile's stay in the facility.

Friendship at Intake

I was the Intake Officer screening the delinquent referrals and setting court dates for adjudicatory hearings when I received the police report on Jesse. Two officers were in the reception area waiting to bring Jesse, a 16-year-old male, to my office. Jesse, two other juveniles, and two adults were apprehended burglarizing a private residence. Jesse was not in the house but was loading stolen articles into a van, which was stolen from another location.

The officers accompanied Jesse into my office and removed the handcuffs and leg irons at my request. They gave me all their paperwork and left. Jesse stood up and looked at the door.

David: "Jesse, I think I need to give you some information that might make things a little easier for you. There is a sheriff's deputy in the reception room. You probably saw him while you were waiting out there. So, any juvenile who shows up out there without an adult with him or her will go straight to jail and will not pass go nor collect $200.00. You dig?"

This statement is neither a threat nor punishment; it is reality and a natural consequence. I will not use external control short of defending myself from physical harm. In short, I will do nothing that will drive this young man and me farther apart. I must connect with him if we are to have any chance of him making some changes in his behavior.

Jesse: "Dig? Gawd, what century you from man? You from outer space?"

David: "That may be true Jesse, but I'm the best alien that you could hope for, trust me on that one."

Jesse: "Why should I trust you? I don't even know you."

David: "That's right Jesse, you don't know me, but I'm fixin' to remedy that right quick. I'm David, and I would appreciate it if you would call me by my first name, 'cause I'm planning on calling you by your first. O.K.?"

Jesse: "I'll call you whatever I damn well please. What you gonna do about that, throw me in detention?"

David: "Jesse, you are going to detention all right but not because I'm going to throw you in there. Let me advance your education just a tiny bit. Any juvenile who is brought in here and is accused of committing a felony is, by law, automatically placed in detention until his adjudicatory hearing. Now, I'm an easy guy to get along with, and I will negotiate with you, deal with you, all that stuff when I can. But when it is the law, there is no negotiation. Understood?"

Jesse: "Yeah. So, now what?"

David: "Look man, you are tough, and that's O.K. I've looked at your record, and you have been to juvie on two other occasions. When you were three, the child welfare put you in a foster home because you were being neglected. That's done. Let's don't even talk about it. Then, when you were ten, you were brought in for stealing a bicycle, and last year, for not attending school. That stuff is already done, and we can't take it back, so we are done with it. What I need to know is the present and future. What are you planning for next year?"

Jesse: "I'll call you collect from the bank before we knock it over."

Jesse started laughing at his own humor. I sat quietly, not laughing but just waiting until he finished.

When things got quiet, I looked at him.

David: "Funny. Oh yeah, funny. Now won't that look good in my intake report? That is not stuff I want to forward to the judge for your adjudicatory hearing. That is stuff that he will look at when it comes to the dispositional hearing. You see Jesse, you may not understand that the judge will most likely adjudicate you a delinquent, and then he will have to decide how good a risk you are for probation. If he decides you are already planning a bank job, most likely you will become a state boy. You know what that means?"

State boy is a well-known term to youth who have been to juvenile court. It means that the court will remove youth from their home and commit them to the state which will decide in which institution they will be placed. I now had Jesse's attention.

Jesse: "Hey! Wait a minute man, I was just jivin' you. C'mon man; don't throw me to the dogs."

David: "Look Jesse, I really don't like the crap you have been involved in. Burglarizing a home, and we will never know how many you helped knock over before you got caught. No, I don't even want to hear you deny or admit that. What I'm interested in is, what do you want to do with your life from now on? I don't know you well, and you don't know me well, but I care enough about you to want to help you get your stuff together. Are you interested?"

Jesse: "I'm goin' to state anyway, what difference does it make? And don't hand me no crap about how you care about me. Nobody cares about me but my granny."

David: "I kinda like grandmas too. Like you, I also had a good one. Tell me about yours."

Jesse looked at me strangely, and then he stared out the window for a little bit. I just waited patiently.

Jesse: "Grams. That's what all us kids call her. I've lived with her since I was eight, and the welfare gave me to her. My mama didn't want me, but my grams did."

I knew from the police report that Jesse was still living with his grandmother. I also knew she had not been in good health since having a stroke less than a year ago.

David: "You must love your grams a lot. Your face really lights up when you talk about her. Where is she now?"

Jesse: "She's home, but she is not very healthy. My sister and I try to take care of her. But, why are you asking me all this stuff man? What's this got to do with anything?"

David: "Look Jesse. This isn't hurting anything if we get to know each other a little bit. My grandmother's name was Lottie. I loved her a lot. She is dead now, but we had some great times. When I was a kid, I visited her and my grandpa once on their farm. There was a skunk that had gotten into their chicken house, and my grams took out after him throwing rocks at him. I helped too, and finally we rocked that old skunk to death, and neither one of us got hit with his stink. Have you ever smelled a skunk?"

Jesse was looking at me strangely again. He could not understand my not using external control with him. He apparently was confused. Often, if an adult self-discloses some of his or her life, the behavior confuses a delinquent. However, self-disclosure goes a long way toward establishing the trust between the staff member and the youth.

Jesse: "You are one strange dude, you know that?"

David: "Why do you say that Jesse?"

Jesse: "I'm in here for burglary, you have the cops take my cuffs off and leave you alone with me, and then you start talking about grandmas and skunks and things. What you up to?"

David: "Oh, about five eight, how tall are you?"

Jesse smiled for the first time, a good sign. I believe that humor can be a very useful tool when used appropriately.

Jesse: "Man, you are giving me a headache. I ain't never laughed in no probation officer's office before."

David: "Look, Jesse, what is wrong with us getting to know each other a little bit? We are both just doing our job. Your job is to be a delinquent and mine is to be a probation officer. Now, I think you haven't done a very good job of being a delinquent. You got caught. My question to you is, would you like to change jobs?"

Jesse: "Delinquency isn't a job, what you talking about?"

David: "O.K. O.K. I won't argue with you, but is being a delinquent what you want to do for the rest of your life? Because if it is, I can help you along by not doing my job. Is that something you think you want?"

Jesse: "Look, it was an accident we got caught."

David: "Well, that accident will put your adult friends away for quite some time, what do you think of that?"

Jesse: "You don't know they'll be put away. We weren't violent. Nobody got hurt."

David: "Oh yeah, I know. Both your friends have records and this lit-
            tle accident, as you call it, will get them under the habitual
            criminal statute which will send them to the slammer fifteen
            to twenty. How old will you be when your friends get out?"

Jesse: "I don't know."

David: "Well, figure it, I saw a report on your grades. You did pretty
            well in math. You are sixteen, now add twenty to that, what
            do you get?"

Jesse thought for a moment, and then his mouth formed an oh, and he let out a
little gush of air.

Jesse: "Gawd! I'll be thirty six; that's an old man!"

David: "And when you are this thirty-six-year-old-man, what will
            you be doing? A job to support a wife and kids, or will you
            also be doing fifteen to twenty, or even life?"

Jesse: "How come you are talking all this stuff. Ain't you suppose to
            be getting testimony, and evidence and all that paper stuff you
            officers do?"

David: "I would rather get to know you better and see if we can be
            friends, even if for the short time we know each other. Is there
            anything wrong with that?"

Jesse: "What does it get me to be friends with you?"

David: "Well, for one thing, it gives you something I don't think you
            have ever had."

Jesse: "Oh, I've had lots of friends. Is that what you mean?"

David: "No, I mean a friend like me. Someone who cares about what
            you do with your life and is willing to help you make things
            better. You see, I don't think you are very happy, and maybe
            you haven't been happy for a long time. How would you like
            to be happy most of the time, not all the time, but most of the
            time. Happy, and not looking over your shoulder to see if
            someone is after you?"

Jesse: "I'm O.K. I don't need nobody. I get along fine."

David: "Jesse, may I ask you one question?"

Jesse looked at me with a suspicious eye. He shuffled in his chair and looked at the floor, then at me.

Jesse: "O.K. One question."

David: "Do you want to stay at Grams or do you want to go to state?"

Jesse: "That is the dumbest question I think I ever heard. You got no sense."

David: "That may be true, but please, answer the question."

Jesse: "I want to stay at Grams, but that judge ain't goin' to let me do that."

David: "Well, he might not, but if he thought about it and asked you, 'What are you willing to do different to stay at Grams?' what will you say?"

Jesse: "I'd say that I'd never steal again."

David: "Oh, you probably said that when you took the bicycle. It will take more than that."

Jesse's face twisted into a snarl, and he answered me sarcastically.

Jesse: "You're so smart, honky, tell me. What do I have to tell the judge?"

Jesse is obviously still looking for me to use criticizing, blaming, complaining, punishing, and threatening to destroy any relationship we are building. His sarcasm is something that I will ignore. It serves no purpose to get into a power struggle over words or name calling. The name calling or vulgar language will not deter me, and I will continue to build on connecting.

David:	"You don't have to tell the judge anything. It is your choice what you do and if you mean what you say you will do."
Jesse:	"I may be bad, but I ain't no liar. If I say I'll do something, my word is good."
David:	"Jesse, I need to ask you something that is very important to you and what happens while you are in juvie. Are you ready?"
Jesse:	"Do I have any choice?"
David:	"Sure, if you are not interested, we are through, and I'll accompany you on up to detention."
Jesse:	"All right. All right. What's the question? You knew I'd do that didn't you?"
David:	"I was hoping you would. My job as the intake counselor is almost over. I have one last thing to do. I must assign you to a probation officer. I have the choice of assigning you to some- one else, or assigning myself as your probation officer. What would you choose that I do?"

For the second time this day, Jesse's mouth dropped open. He just stared at me in disbelief.

Jesse:	"Are you serious? You'll let me decide who my probation officer will be? What happens if I choose you?"
David:	"We get to know each other a little more, and when we go to court, I will share with the judge what has been going on, and what I think would be in your best interest and also the com- munity's best interest. I will never lie to you. After we work together for a bit, if I think it would be best for the state to help you, that is what I will tell you and the judge. I'll always be up front. But if you choose another officer, he will also tell the judge what he thinks is best for you and for the communi- ty. That answer your question?"
Jesse:	"Hell, you're not such a bad dude , I'll go with you."

Jesse was adjudicated delinquent. At his dispositional hearing, the judge grant-
ed him probation, with home detention where he was monitored with an electronic leg strap. He was admonished that if there was another referral of any
kind, there would be no hearing. He would be transported forthwith to the state.

I saw Jesse for four months, and the electronic device was removed. His school
work improved, and he was able to work part-time at McDonald's. Jesse was
released from probation in the middle of his senior year. When he graduated
from high school, he entered the local community college. Later, he went to the
state university where he began work on becoming a teacher. I've lost track of
Jesse through the years, but I'm confident he is well.

The above scenario may seem too simple, too easy; just eliminate external control and make friends with him. You also may be thinking that if the process is
this easy, why aren't all corrections people doing it?

We know that building a relationship will be exceptionally difficult for you to
do the first time. Everything you have been taught as a corrections worker is to
control delinquents, make them conform to the rules. If you let them get away
with misbehavior, they will get worse, not better, and they will continue a life of
crime. They must "own up to their crimes" and pay for what they have done.
But if you can eliminate the deadly habits, the improved relationship will make
your job easier and more enjoyable. At first, you are not going to be comfortable because you have been using external control all of your life. You will need
to avoid giving up and keep practicing.

The best way to learn this new way, Choice Theory, and feel more comfortable
using it, is to change your way of life outside the job—especially with your family and friends. Examine how you treat your friends the next time you are
together. The deadly habits are absent, along with external control, except when
you are joking. This occurs because our friends will terminate the friendship if
we try to "make" them do something they don't want to do. The same is true if
our friends try to make us do something we don't want to do. Just treat the youth

you work with as you do your family and friends. This practice will not be easy because you have been using external control all your life.

We have worked with youth for over 45 years, and we have seen an array of treatment models used in the rehabilitation of delinquents. We are convinced that there is one thing absolutely essential to obtaining the most from any approach. That "thing" is making friends with juveniles and building a relationship with them.

Why is friendship so important? Friendship elicits trust, which is a result of satisfying the strong love and belonging need we have. Friendship has its risks. There are counterfeits in friendship, which shouldn't surprise us, because anything as valuable as friendship is sure to encourage counterfeiting.

Friendship comes in various shapes and sizes. When we promote making friends with delinquents, we are not referring to a holiday card list of friends. We also are not talking about shopping friends, sports buddies, service club friends, religious classmates or other types of ongoing relationships. We are talking about friends similar to friends-in-passing, which is more than a relationship with the person who does our dry cleaning or scans our groceries. The big difference is that making friends with juveniles means relating that you care about them. You must communicate with juveniles that although you do not approve of their criminal acts, you care about the juveniles as human beings.

Jim, a director of adult detention, attended one of David's training classes. Jim said that he "didn't feel he could be friends with the inmates."

Jim: "I can't be friends with these guys in here. A friend to me is someone I would invite to my house for dinner."

David: "I would agree if that is the definition that we must use for friendship."

Upon further questioning, I discovered that we were pretty close together when we explored the semantics of friendship.

Jim:	"I treat them with respect. I treat them fairly and firmly, and let them know that I care about what they are going to do from now on with their lives."
David:	"So you let them know that you care for them as human beings?"
Jim:	"I tell them as long as they follow the rules, I will go to bat for them and that I care about how they are treated."
David:	"Would you say you arrive at a point where they have some trust in you?"
Jim:	"Yeah. I never thought of it quite like that, but yeah, they do trust me. I'm hard on them if they break the rules, but they know I will be fair."
David:	"Sounds good Jim. I think we are on the same playing field; we just may not use the same name for what we do. Would you agree on that?"
Jim:	"Yeah, I can agree on that, but I'm still not inviting any of them to dinner."

A rose is a rose by any other name. (Gertrude Stein)

By being friendly with the delinquents we work with, we are also modeling and teaching them courtesy, thoughtfulness, kindness and empathy— all social skills they need to learn. So, why not try it? If it doesn't work for you, will you be any worse off than you are now?

Summary

Developing a relationship with juveniles is critical to the success of Reality Therapy and helping juveniles change their behaviors. The key to a good relationship with juveniles is being friendly with them—cooperating, respecting, caring, sharing and listening. The foundation of the relationship is trust, which must be earned. Being open and honest, sharing your interests, and maintaining ethical standards are ways to earn juveniles' trust. All of these require appropriate communication, including listening, a skill that you must develop and practice daily.

Questions

1. List the three steps of involvement that help you build a relationship with juveniles.

   _____

   _____

   _____

2. Define the following terms.
   Tolerance

   _____

   _____

   Respect

   _____

   _____

Cooperation

_____

_____

3. List at least five listening faults.

_____

_____

_____

_____

_____

4. What are two questions that you should ask yourself to ensure that you are listening appropriately to juveniles?

_____

_____

5. Listening to the total message means listening to both the _____ and _____ parts of the message.

6. List four traits that you need to teach Reality Therapy.

• _____

• _____

• _____

• _____

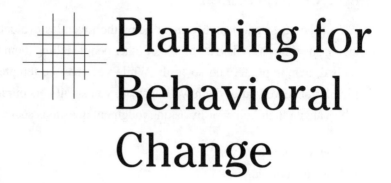 # Planning for Behavioral Change

Objectives

After reading this chapter, you will be able to:

- Describe how to help juveniles evaluate their own behavior
- Describe how to make a plan
- List seven traits of a good plan
- Explain how to make a contract

In this chapter, we will discuss Steps 7-10 of involvement:

- Step 7: Have juveniles evaluate their own behavior.
- Step 8: Help juveniles work out a plan.
- Step 9: Make a contract.

When we evaluate juveniles' behavior, they get defensive. When we help them evaluate their own behavior, we provide an opportunity for growth. Without their defensiveness, we can help them work out a plan and agree on a contract about what choices to make next time.

Step 7 of Involvement

Step 7 of the 13 steps of involvement helps the juveniles evaluate their own behavior. Juveniles have had a lifetime of other people telling them their behavior is bad, inappropriate, and so forth. While you may be tempted, lecturing them will not serve you or them well. Instead, you should encourage juveniles to self-evaluate their behavior by asking judgment questions such as:

- How will this help you?
- What is your plan?
- Did this help you accomplish your goal or plan?
- Are you doing right or wrong?
- Is this something you are proud of—something you would want others to know you did?
- Is this something you would want your sister or brother to do?
- When did you decide to do this?
- Are you acting responsibly?
- Will doing this help you be released early?
- Will doing this help you stay out of trouble?
- Will this help you accomplish what you want to accomplish?

Let's look at the scenario of Chad, 16-years-old, and his family. We will see how David gets them to look at their behavior, evaluate it, and make plans on behaving differently.

Chad lives at home with his father, stepmother and two half-sisters, ages six and eight. This visit is my first one to their home. Chad was assigned to me, and as his probation officer, I scheduled an initial meeting with him and his parents at their home.

When I arrived, Chad's stepmother answered the door.

David:	"Good morning, I'm David Jackson. I'm Chad's probation officer. May I talk with Chad, you and your husband for a few minutes?"
Mrs. T:	"I'm glad you are here. I need for you to get him out of this house or to make him mind me before I kill him!"
David:	"Mrs. T, I can't make your son do anything he doesn't want to do. I just kind of wanted to meet all of you, get to know each other, and see what we can do together to make things better."
Mrs. T:	"If you can't make him mind what am I suppose to do? And, I'm not his mother; I'm his stepmother. I'd like to give him to his mother if she were around. Lord knows where she took off to, but I'd like to join her just to get away from both of them. I'm going to leave them again. I told him I would if he didn't make that kid behave."
David:	"May I come in Mrs. T? I would like to talk to all of you if that is all right."
Mrs. T:	"Yeah, sure, I'm sorry, where are my manners? The girls are visiting my sister. It's all the worry I have over that kid. I tell you he and his father are driving me crazy. I sure hope you can straighten this mess out."

I followed Mrs. T into the living room where Chad and his father were sitting on the couch watching television.

| Mrs. T: | "Turn that damn thing off. Mr. Jackson from the juvenile hall is here to talk to Chad." |

No one moved to turn the television off. They just looked up at me, nodded, and returned to watching the tube. I walked over to the couch and held my hand out to Chad and then his father as I introduced myself. I experienced two "wet noodles" for handshakes.

David: "Would you mind if we turn your TV off for just a while so we can talk about Chad staying out of jail, or spending more time there?"

When I said jail, Chad moved quickly to the TV and turned it off.

Chad: "Why would I have to go to jail? I ain't never been in trouble before this, and it wasn't my fault this time. The keys were in that there car. If you leave your keys in your car, you are asking for someone to borrow it. Right?"

David: "Right? I don't think the court agreed with you. If they had, would you now be on probation?"

When I asked this question, Chad's father looked at me for the first time.

Mr. T: "Chad is a good boy. He just got in with the wrong crowd."

David: "Wasn't Chad alone when he took the car?"

Mr. T: "Yeah, but you have to remember he had just gotten out of the state hospital. He was under a lot of stress."

Mrs. T: "Oh sure, see. His father is always making excuses for him. They should never have let him out of the hospital. He came home and started doing the same stuff as before. You know, kicking the furniture whenever he loses it, and knocking holes in the wall. See that hole over there? Chad did that."

Chad: "That was over a year ago. I don't do that anymore."

I sat just listening to the diatribe between each of the family members. I decided to start asking some more value questions. Value questions help clients get on their thinking wheel instead of on their feeling wheel. Such questions help clients self-evaluate their present behavior. They can examine whether their behavior is taking them in the right direction, and if not, how they can change their behavior to go in a different direction.

David:	"Do you, Mrs. T, and you, Mr. T, want Chad to remain living at home?"
Mrs. T:	"I don't. He has driven me up the wall, and I'm ready to leave. But I'm sure his father wants him to stay."
David:	"Well, Mr. T can answer for himself. How about it Mr. T?"

Mr. T just nodded, and then Chad spoke up.

Chad:	"I don't know why I would have to not stay here. I like it. The hospital was the pits, and if she would stay off my back, I wouldn't have any problems."
David:	"If Chad continues the behavior that brought him to the juvenile court's attention, do you think he has much of a chance of living at home? I'll ask you first Mr. T"
Mr. T:	"Well, if she would stay off his back, he'll be all right. He's just a normal kid having growing pains. He'll be all right."
Ms. T:	"I'm leaving, I'm leaving. I've told him before I am going to leave if this crap keeps up. I mean it this time."
David:	"It sounds like you have threatened to leave before, is that correct Mrs. T?"
Mrs. T:	"I did leave him once. So yes, you could say I mean it."
David:	"When you left before, why did you return?"
Mrs. T:	"Oh, he came after me and begged me to come home. He was hungry I think. Neither one of them can boil water."
David:	"So you left once, and now you are threatening to do it again?"
Mrs. T:	"I'm not just threatening. I am going to do it if they don't get their act together."
David:	"Mrs. T, when will you leave? Do you have a plan?"

Mrs. T:	"Why yes. Soon."
David:	"What does soon look like? Tonight? Tomorrow? Next week? What is your time frame?"
Mrs. T:	"Well ... in a month. Yes. In a month. If things aren't better in a month, I'm out of here. As the kids say, I'm history."
David:	"Let's set a firm date right now, so we know what time frame we have to work in. This is September the 10th. So, are you going to leave on October the 10th if things aren't better?"
Mrs. T:	"Yes. October the 10th. I'm going to my sister's, and I won't be coming back no matter how much he begs me this time."

The purpose of pressing for a date is to:

- help Mrs. T get away from one of the deadly habits (threatening), and
- set some firm structure to work toward a plan to make things better.

David:	"So, if things can be better, you might consider staying. Is that what I hear you saying?"
Mrs. T:	"Yes, if he will get off the sofa and do some stuff, and Chad would start doing some things around here instead of kicking everything, I would consider staying."
David:	"Mr. T, do you want your wife to stay or leave?"

For the first time, Mr. T spoke with some emotion.

Mr. T:	"I want her to stay but only if she stops nagging. Nag, nag, nag, it never ends. Chad is just a growing boy. He will be all right if we just leave him alone."
David:	"Had he been left alone when he stole the car Mr. T?"
Mr. T:	"Well, that was a mistake, I admit, but, Chad has learned his lesson. What do you want us to do?"

David: "I'll tell you Mr. T. If Mrs. T leaves as she has promised she will do on October 10, if things don't get better, I can guarantee you, Chad won't make it here. He will most likely go back into the hospital or some other juvenile facility. Is that what you want?"

Mr. T: "No, I don't."

Chad sat up straight on the sofa.

Chad: "I sure don't want that. I want to stay home. If she would stay off my back, I will be all right."

Mrs. T: "See, it's my fault. He always blames me for everything that goes wrong. It's never the kid's fault. I'm sick of it. I'm just going to leave one of these days."

David: "Whoa, wait a minute. I thought we had established the time frame. Are you leaving in one month if things are not better or are you not?"

Mrs. T: "Yes that's right. I am."

David: "Now, let me understand. You want to stay if it is better, is that correct?"

Mrs. T: "Yes, but it will have to be a hell of a lot better."

Mr. T: "See, there she is, always blaming the boy."

Chad: "Yeah, she picks on me a lot."

Mrs. T: "See, I might as well leave now. They always support each other against me."

David: "I'm not here to referee your arguments, but I will help you make a plan for your relationships to be better. Are all of you interested? If you are not, then there is nothing I can do, and Mrs. T might as well pack her bags for October 10th, and Chad might as well pack his."

Each member of the family sat quietly, and then one by one agreed to make things better.

Mrs. T: "He wants me to stay because he can't take care of the girls, and he sure can't make Chad mind."

David: "O.K. I want to ask each of you what you are willing to do to make things better. Who would like to go first?"

No one spoke or moved. Finally, Chad spoke up.

Chad: "I'll do whatever it takes to stay home. Just tell me what to do."

Mrs. T: "I could tell him what he could do."

David: "Chad, are you willing to hear what your stepmother suggests?"

Chad: "Yeah."

David: "What would you suggest Mrs. T?"

Mrs. T: "He could do the chores he is suppose to do and not put his fist through the walls anymore when he loses it."

David: "What chores are you talking about?"

Mrs. T: "He is supposed to take the trash out each week, and wash the dishes on Tuesday and Thursday nights."

David: "Does that sound reasonable to you Chad?"

Chad: "Yeah, I can do that."

David: "We know you can do that, but you haven't been doing it have you? So, what will make it different this time?"

Chad: "I know if I don't, I may get sent away."

David: "That's good thinking Chad. Can you also keep your fists out of the wall?"

Chad: "Oh yeah. I haven't hit the wall in over a year. I can handle that."

David: "Yes, we know you can but will you?"

Chad:	"Yes, I will. And I'll do the chores too. All those things are going to be hard to remember."
David:	"O.K. We'll make a list of those things you have agreed to do and pin them to the wall here by the refrigerator where they will be easy for you to see and help remind you. O.K.?"
Chad:	"O.K."
David:	"How about you Mr. T? What will you do to make things better?"

Mr. T suddenly lost his powers of speech, so Mrs. T spoke up.

Mrs. T:	"I know what he could do. He could get his butt off that couch and take the girls out once in awhile so I could have some time to myself."
David:	"Where would you be willing to take your daughters Mr. T?"
Mr. T:	"I'm awfully tired when I get home from work. It will be difficult."
David:	"Do you work on weekends Mr. T?"
Mr. T:	"Well, no."
David:	"Then, you could take your daughters to the park on Saturday and Sunday couldn't you?"
Mr. T:	"Well, yes, but the grass might need mowing."
David:	"Chad, are you willing to mow the grass so your father can take your sisters to the park, or would you rather help him with the girls at the park?"
Chad:	"Yes, yes, I will do that. I sure don't want to have to go to the park with them."
David:	"How does that sound Mr. T?"
Mr. T:	"Yeah, I can do that. I want to be back to watch the football game in the afternoon."
David:	"So, what time will you take the girls to the park in order to be back for the football game?"

Mr. T:	"I can take them right after breakfast."
David:	"Mrs. T, if he takes the girls to the park on Saturday and Sunday after breakfast, will that please you?"
Mrs. T:	"God yes! I'll probably have a heart attack. But will he do it?"
David:	"We don't know that. We will see. O.K. Now, Mrs. T, what are you willing to do to make it all better?"
Mrs. T:	"Well, I'll cook their meals."
David:	"You've been doing that haven't you?"
Mrs. T:	"Well, yes."
David:	"I mean something new and ongoing that will make things better."
Chad:	"I know what she could do."
Mrs. T:	"Here we go again."
David:	"Well, Mrs. T, Chad agreed to listen to your suggestion, do you think you might listen to what he has to say?"
Mrs. T:	"Oh, all right, but I'm not saying I'll do what he comes up with."
David:	"Well, what do you think Chad might come up with?"
Mrs. T:	"He's always complaining about my bitching, so he'll probably harp on that."

Chad was nodding his head vigorously.

David:	"Mrs. T, do you think the bitching is a problem?"
Mrs. T:	"I probably could stop griping so much, but it is hard when one's on the couch and the other is lying on the floor watching the boob tube all the time."
David:	"May I make a suggestion?"
Mrs. T:	"Yeah, yeah, O.K."
David:	"Instead of nagging at Chad about his chores, just point to his list. How about that?"
Mrs. T:	"That's a good idea. I'll do that."

David:	"And if Chad doesn't need prodding and does some on his own, what might you say?"
Mrs. T:	"Oh that will be the day."
David:	"But when that day arrives, what might you say to him."
Mrs. T:	"I could thank him. Lord, I can't believe I said that."
David:	"Will you do that?"
Mrs. T:	"Yes, yes, if he will take some responsibility, I'll do that."
David:	"Now, may I make another suggestion?"
Mrs. T:	"Yes, of course, go ahead."
David:	"Write that down on Chad's list. Just print 'thank you,' and that will remind you when he does it, you can thank him. Will you do that?"
Mrs. T:	"Yes, I can do that. It probably will remind me to remember."
David:	"O.K.? Now Chad, if she points at the list instead of bitching, and thanks you when you do those things on your own, will you like that?"
Chad:	"Oh yeah. But I'll probably have a heart attack too."
David:	"Well, if you do, your stepmother can call the doctor."
Mrs. T:	"Yeah. Wow, this is certainly something new. I never thought anything like this would happen when you came through that door today."
David:	"We don't know, but you all three have come up with some real good ideas. If you do what each of you has said he and she will do, things will be better, and both of you, Mrs. T and you Chad, can unpack your bags and plan on staying home."

Now let's look at using value questions with Jamal, a hard-core delinquent arrested for murder.

I first met Jamal in the detention center. He was 17 and was going to his adjudication for shooting two other young men in a drive-by shooting. Jamal was unresponsive at our first meeting and declared that he did not care what happened to him.

The second meeting with Jamal started off much the same as the first had.

David: "Hi Jamal, how is it going today?"

Jamal: "Same as everyday in this stinking place. So you can quit asking."

David: "Oh, I'll continue to ask because I care."

Jamal: "Look, I already confessed to the pigs, so what are you hounding me for?"

David: "Because it's my job, Jamal, and I would like to help you make the best of a bad situation."

Jamal: "Make the best of what?"

David: "Look Jamal, what would you like to see happen under the circumstances?"

Jamal: "Just send me up and get it over with, that's all I got to say."

David: "I know one thing for sure. (I waited for Jamal to respond.)"

Jamal: "O.K. I'll bite. What you know for sure?"

David: "I know that you are unhappy, and that's exactly what I would be too. I don't know anyone who wouldn't be in your case. But that's where you and I differ. (I waited again.)"

Jamal: "You gonna tell me the difference, or do I have to go through my whole life wondering my goodness, I wonder what it is?"

David: "I would grasp at any idea that might make it not as bad."

Jamal: "Look, Jackson, I wasted two dudes who had it coming, but that don't make no difference to no judge. He's going to certify me as an adult and going to burn me, and that's for sure."

David: "Yeah, there is no death penalty in this state, so he will probably send you to prison. But if there was something that would make the rest of your life just a tiny bit better, would you be interested?"

Jamal stopped and stared at me. He slowly got up out of his chair and turned to the window. I heard him take a deep breath. Then, he turned to me and spoke.

Jamal: "Look man, if I could turn back the clock, that would make it better. Yeah, if there was something else I would listen."

David: "What is past is past, and we can't change that, but when you go to the place the judge decides upon, I know some things that might help make it just a little better. Are you interested?"

Jamal: "Yeah, I guess so, but I don't really care anymore."

David: (I decided to take a different tact.) "Jamal, what kinds of things do you like other than drugs, stealing, and shooting each other?"

Jamal: (Bristling.) "You smart bastard. You think that's all we do in my neighborhood? Don't you think I care about anything else?"

Jamal has chosen angering with me, and when he does, his depression disappears. Choice Theory says that we choose depressing to control our angering. In my experience, when we choose angering, it is difficult to also depress.

David: (I'm now trying to keep him on his thinking wheel.) "What else do you care about Jamal?"

Jamal: "I care about my little sister and my mother. I care about what happens to my friends, and I like to draw and ride motorcycles. I even started liking to read some things in school before I got in this trouble."

David: "You have just told me that you have other interests. Well, you can have some other interests in a locked place that you may go to. It is up to you to create some interests just like you were doing at home."

Jamal: "Now how in the hell can I do that behind bars and a 14-foot barbed wire fence?"

David:	"You ever been to a library?"
Jamal:	"You ask some of the dumbest questions. You must think I'm a retard."
David:	"No, but that seems to be the only way I can get you to talk with me, is to piss you off or insult you. I'd rather you see me as a friend trying to help you make the best of a bad situation."
Jamal:	"Why do you give a shit what happens to me? You don't even know me."
David:	"All that is quite true, but that's why I'm talking with you. I'm trying for us to get to know each other. Is there anything wrong with that?"
Jamal:	(Thinks for a few seconds.) "No … I guess not. It's just that I've never had a white guy ever care anything about what happens to me."
David:	"Why limit it to white? Have you ever had any man want to be your friend?"
Jamal:	(He turned away from me and thought for a long time.) "I ain't no homo, but I sometimes have wished that my dad hadn't left us, not that I really care, but I just sometimes think about it."
David:	"Look Jamal, if you considered me a friend, this is what that friend would say to you now. Would you like to get your high school diploma while you are locked up?"
Jamal:	"Yeah, I guess so, but how can I do that?"
David:	"You know what the GED is?"
Jamal:	"Yeah, can you do that in prison?"
David:	"Not only that, but lots of guys have gone on after completing their GED and taken college courses. Even gotten college degrees. It is really up to you. What do you think?"
Jamal:	"How would I find out about all this shit?"
David:	"Wherever you go, there will be an orientation officer, and you can get that information from him or from the chaplain."

Reality Therapy and Choice Theory

I saw Jamal twice more prior to his court hearing. I continued to reinforce the Choice Theory idea with him, especially that he could control only his behavior and no one else's. Jamal was certified as an adult and eventually sentenced to 20 years in prison. I gave Jamal all any of us can give each other—friendship and information. What each of us does with that information is our responsibility.

Steps 8 and 9 of Involvement

When juveniles admit their behavior is not helping them accomplish their goals or meet their needs, the next phase of RT begins: making better choices. The next two steps move us into making better choices.

8. Help the juvenile work out a plan.
9. Make a contract.

After you have determined that the juveniles realize and accept that their previous behavior has not helped them meet their needs, you should ask this question: "What will you do the next time?" Do not accept one answer. Make a list and write them on paper. Help the juveniles explore all the options available by asking, "What else could you do?" Help them brainstorm the options by offering suggestions yourself. Ask, "Could you do ... ?" Remember that one of the options available would be to do the same thing over again.

You might say, "I'm a line officer and don't have time to this," or "I'm a line officer, not a counselor." Our answer would be that 80 percent of treatment and teaching is done by you. And, you will be spending less time doing this than you would with discipline, restrictions, and corrective action over and over.

Robert E. Wubbolding, Ph.D., and Janet A. Thatcher, Ph.D., in their *Reality Therapy Training Intensive Workshop Training Workbook*, list 13 traits of a good plan:

1. Simple
2. Attainable
3. Measurable, exact, precise
4. Short-range
5. Immediate
6. Controlled by the doer of the plan
7. Repetitive
8. Able to be revised
9. Personal
10. Positive
11. Evaluated
12. Process centered vs. outcome centered
13. Want and need fulfilling

Let's look at the scenario of Lisa and see how David helps her make a plan. Lisa, a 12-year-old girl, was sent to an open institution cottage by a juvenile court for stealing, truancy and running away.

Mrs. Parker, Lisa's 6th grade English teacher, asked me to talk with Lisa if she was returned to the institution. When Mrs. Parker asked her to stay after class and explain why she wasn't doing her homework, Lisa threw her books on the floor of the classroom. Then, she ran from the classroom and the campus. Staff contacted the police and, within an hour, they apprehended Lisa and returned her to the main office of the institution. The office staff walked her back to the school building and to her teacher, Mrs. Parker, who placed her in the time out room. This is the third time Lisa has run from the campus. Each time, the police returned her within one to six hours after she had left. Mrs. Parker indicated she was "at her wit's end." As we discussed Lisa, Mrs. Parker said to me. "I have tried punishing the girl to no avail. I've talked until I'm blue in the face. At this point, I will try anything to get Lisa to straighten up. Can you help us? The whole institution is upset with her."

David: I listened to Mrs. Parker, then answered her.
                      "I'll talk with Lisa and see what we can come up with.
                      I haven't any magic, but we shall see. You indicate you are
                      willing to try something different with Lisa, is that correct?"

Mrs. Parker: "Oh yes, yes, but I don't know what it could be."

David: "I don't either, but let's see if Lisa can come up with some-
                      thing that would be agreeable with all the parties involved."

Lisa was sitting in the time out room of the school by herself when I entered. She was slumped over a desk and glanced at me when I entered and then looked away.

David: "Hi Lisa, I'm David, may I talk with you for a few minutes?"

No answer. Lisa just stared down at the desk where she was seated.

David: "I just wanted to talk, that's all, because I figured you to be
                      pretty unhappy right now, and maybe together we can find a
                      way for you to be happier. Would you like that?"

Lisa: Lisa never looked up but said, "I don't have to talk to you or
                      anybody else if I don't want to."

David: "You are absolutely right, but if you will let me, I would like
                      to be your friend and just chat with you a little. Is that all right
                      with you?"

Lisa: "Hell no! Just leave me alone. I'm not saying another word."

I tried talking a little more, but she paid no attention, just sat slumped over the desk and stared at the wall in front of her.

David: "Is there anything you would like to ask me or talk about?"

There was no response.

"Lisa, since you have never met me and know nothing about me, let me tell you a little about who I am and what I do. If that is O.K. with you just keep staring at the wall. You don't have to say a thing to me, O.K.?"

Lisa continued staring at the wall and said nothing.

"Thank you for letting me explain about myself. I travel around the country and try to make things better for young people like you. Would you like for things to be better here for you? If you would, just stay real still and continue looking at the wall. Thank you, this is going just fine. Now, you don't have to say a thing. I'll just chat with you and see if you and I can make things better. Now, to make things better, would things need to be different for you in the school classroom? If I'm on the right track, just keep sitting quietly at your desk. Good! Let's see now, what can I ask you that might help make things better?"

Lisa shuffled in her chair and started staring out the window.

"Now Lisa, if I understand correctly, the homework might be something you would like to be better, is that correct? Just keep staring out the window if that is correct, O.K.? Good, I think we are making some headway here. Thank you for communicating with me."

Lisa, said nothing, took a deep breath, then sat up straight and laced her hands behind her head, staring straight ahead at the wall.

"I guess I would like to know if you like doing homework or do not like it. My guess is that you don't like it. If that is wrong, just lift your forefinger of your right hand. Good, I'm correct then in my assumption."

Lisa turned and glared at me.

Lisa:	"How f***ing long are you going to go on with this shit?"
David:	"I'm sorry, I'm just trying to be friendly, and I thought maybe these were some things that were contributing to your unhappiness."
Lisa:	"I'm not unhappy! Everything is cool, O.K.?"
David:	"If things are cool for you now, how could they be even cooler?"
Lisa:	"Parker would drop dead. That's how they could be cooler."
David:	"What would be different in your life if Parker dropped dead?"
Lisa:	"There would be no more embarrassing me in front of the whole class."
David:	"I remember once when a teacher embarrassed me in front of everyone."

As part of connecting with a young client, I have found that self-disclosure is helpful. Self-disclosure lends itself toward showing trust, and if you show trust, it encourages the client to reciprocate.

Lisa:	"Big deal." I just sat quietly for a few seconds, and then Lisa broke the silence. "O.K. big shot, what happened?"
David:	"Well, I was in the third grade, and the teacher had stepped out of the room for some reason, so I picked up my book and hit a little friend of mine on the head with it. The teacher was looking in another door window and saw me."

I waited again a few seconds.

Lisa:	"Well ... what happened? Did she chew you out in front of the class?"
David:	"No, she came in and grabbed me by the collar and put me over her knee. Then she gave me a few good licks with her hand."
Lisa:	"Well, you deserved that for hitting the other kid. I never hit any of the other kids in my class."
David:	"If you don't hit the other kids, what do you do with them?"
Lisa:	"I don't mess with them. I just leave everybody alone. I don't need anyone."
David:	"Do you have any friends?"
Lisa:	"No. Who needs friends?"
David:	"If you ever decided that you were going to have a friend, what would he or she have to be like?"
Lisa:	A long time expired before Lisa finally spoke again. "Well, it wouldn't be a boy, for sure. It would be a girl, and she would have to not talk all the time, but listen to what I think is important, and she would be honest and a loyal friend even when I acted like a bitch. We would share clothes and other stuff. Oh, hell, I don't know, what's the use of talking about it?"
David:	"Wow, that sounds like the kind of friends I like. Especially the listening part. It feels good when someone thinks that what I say is important. How about you?"
Lisa:	"Yeah, I guess that's it. Important."

Then Lisa was quiet, thinking.

David:	"When do you feel important here Lisa?"

Lisa turned and stared at me.

Power is a very important genetic need, and very difficult for youth to satisfy in this kind of a setting, especially in classrooms. An understanding teacher, one who attempts to make friends with her students, is necessary. Listening is an important way for any staff member to help youth satisfy their need for power.

Lisa: "Are you for real? There is nothing here to feel important about, and you're crazy if you think there is."

She stared out the window some more.

David: "What would it feel like if you and I could create or think of something that you would feel important about?"

These self-evaluation questions are very important, especially at this juncture, because we are obviously accomplishing some connecting with each other.

Lisa: Finally, Lisa turned slowly in her chair and looked at me, then turned away. "That would be impossible here."

David: "If you had a magic WANT, and could do the impossible here, what would you wish for to feel important?"

I emphasized want instead of wand because I can sense Lisa starting to slip back into her shell. I ask her something to help her stay on the thinking component of her total behavior.

Lisa: "You need some help from Parker. It's wand, not want. What a dummy. And they think I'm dumb."

This retort was different. Lisa grinned as she spoke to me. I smiled back. Humor is good. It means that there is some fun present, and fun is generally accompanied with learning. Maybe Lisa is beginning to learn some things. Let's see.

David:	"No, really. I mean a want! What would be one of your big wants to happen while you are here that wouldn't get you in trouble?"
Lisa:	"Well, it's no big deal, but if I could get out of doing homework, I would be happy."
David:	"How many days are you told to do homework now?"
Lisa:	"Every day, Monday, Tuesday, Wednesday, Thursday and stupid Friday."
David:	"What kind of homework are you asked to do?"
Lisa:	"It's always a chapter in this stupid old book we are reading on warfare. God I hate it!"
David:	"Since you don't like warfare books, what kind of books do you like?"
Lisa:	Lisa thought for a while. "Anything but that shit Parker gives us. Why can't we read about animals or something cool, like clothes?"
David:	"If you were reading about animals, would you be willing to do a chapter a day of homework?"
Lisa:	"Sure, but it'll never happen. Parker would never give us anything to read about stuff I like."
David:	"Have you ever asked Mrs. Parker if you could read about animals?"
Lisa:	"Are you kidding? She would never allow me to do anything I want to."
David:	"If she did, would you be willing to do the work and not run away?"

This is a crucial time in our discussion. I'm putting forth the idea of Lisa doing something different. But I will never use external control. Notice, there are never any "should" statements. A should statement is a battle word to these youth. (It is also a battle word in many families.)

Lisa:	Lisa looked at me incredulously and shook her head. "Yeah, but it'll never happen. Will it?"

This is the first real evidence that Lisa is willing to do something different. This is the result of the hard work of connecting with a difficult child.

David:	"We don't know, but if you were willing to do it, I could ask Mrs. Parker if she would be interested in trying it. Do you want me to check it out?"
Lisa:	Lisa sat up straight in her chair and faced me. "Yeah, but I won't hold my breath. Parker is after me, she doesn't like me at all, ya know?"
David:	"Well, in all honesty, you probably haven't given her much to like. Would that be a fair statement?"
Lisa:	Lisa looked at me and laughed. "You got that right. I figured I might as well have some fun; there was nothing else in the class of interest."
David:	"Well Lisa, are you willing to sign a contract with me stating that you would be willing to read a book on animals and do the assignments that Mrs. Parker gives you and, second, not run away from the place. In return, I will talk with Mrs. Parker and see if she would be willing to go along with your new plan?"
Lisa:	"Yeah, yeah, I'll sign it, but watch out for Parker."
David:	"Oh? Do you think she might make me stay in for recess?"
Lisa:	Lisa stared at me for a moment, then broke out in laughter.
David:	"Hey, that sounds great, you should try that more often."

I wrote up the contract on a piece of paper and signed it and handed it to Lisa. She turned her back to me and leaned over the contract on her desk and began to sign it. I could just barely hear what she said as she signed the paper.

Lisa:	"I feel like a real person."
David:	I found Mrs. Parker at her desk between classes. "Hi, Mrs. Parker, I'm finished talking with Lisa."
Mrs. Parker:	"Is she gone again?"
David:	"No, no. We had a good conversation, and I think we arrived at some new things. Did you mean it when you told me you would do anything to help the situation?"

Mrs. Parker looked at me suspiciously.

Mrs. Parker:	"What has that statement gotten me into?"
David:	"If you are in agreement, Lisa will be allowed to read something different from the present material that I understand is on warfare."

Parker was aghast.

Mrs. Parker:	"You mean give in to her and let her decide what she will read and what she will not read?"
David:	"No, not at all, if what is going on in class now is working. Is it?"
Mrs. Parker:	"No, you know that, but that is the fault of the child. All the other students do the work I assign, why should Lisa be treated as a prima donna?"
David:	"Aside from whose at fault and a prima donna, if Lisa could be persuaded to take part in your class, not have tantrums, not run away, would that be something you would welcome as an improvement?"
Mrs. Parker:	"This is some of that new stuff, that Choice Theory and Reality Therapy stuff isn't it?"

David:	"If what is going on in your class is not working now, wouldn't it make sense to do something different regardless of the name of it?"
Mrs. Parker:	"Well, I guess so. But this is really hard for me to accept!"
David:	"Look Mrs. Parker, you are obviously an excellent teacher with the majority of the kids who are in your class. If you try this new thing and it doesn't work, are you any worse off with Lisa than you are now?"
Mrs. Parker:	She smiled and looked at me. "You are a very persuasive gentleman. You are right, it is not good now, and no it can't be any worse, so, O.K. we'll try it for two weeks. But I will warn you right now, if Lisa doesn't show some improvement, we are going back to the old way."
David:	"What will Lisa need to do so that you feel it is an improvement?"
Mrs. Parker:	"O.K. Do her assignment. No more throwing books and running away. That would be sufficient."
David:	"If it's all right with you Mrs. Parker, I will help Lisa pick out an animal book, and we will bring it by this afternoon for your approval."

Mrs. Parker agreed, and I revisited Lisa and explained what had transpired. I told Lisa that Mrs. Parker would try this plan for two weeks and then reevaluate it to see if it could be continued or not. Lisa was delighted, and we went to the library to select a book.

After two weeks, Mrs. Parker indicated that she was pleased with the change in attitude that Lisa had made. Lisa selected another book and agreed to read some of the new book Mrs. Parker had started the class on, *To Kill a Mockingbird*. This example shows how children can make better choices when:

- minimum external control is used on the youth, and
- they believe that what is being asked of them will be useful in their lives.

Once you and the juveniles have listed all of the options, ask the juveniles to self-evaluate which option would be the best to meet their needs and goals. Do not assume that you have a contract because the juveniles say what they could do the next time. We can all do things that are in our best interest which we never get around to doing. We could lose 10 pounds, or we could exercise more, or we could eat better. The fact that we could do something doesn't mean that we will do it.

To move into a contract, we need to ask the juvenile: "What will you do the next time?" Write this down in the form of a contract and have the juvenile and yourself sign and date it.

The contract should be:

SHORT-TERM: For the next 24 hours.
STATED IN POSITIVE TERMS: I will.
SPECIFIC: Do what the juvenile careworkers ask me to do.

However, 24 hours may be too long. A contract may be: "During study time today, I will do all of my homework for tomorrow." Or, "I will study for 10 minutes tonight." Do not sign a contract that says "I will always" or "For the rest of my life, I will ..."

The juvenile's behavior will not change overnight. Instead, RT usually causes a gradual change in behavior from irresponsible to responsible. Accept small increments of improvement. Studying 10 minutes may not seem like much but if the juvenile has not been studying at all, you have just greatly improved his or her behavior. You then will be ready to move to 15 minutes or more.

We can't accept a contract that allows behavior which is unacceptable. For example, we can't accept a contract that says: "I will only steal 5 cars instead of the 20 that I have been stealing." We also can't accept a contract that continues behavior which is dangerous or injurious to the juvenile or others. For example, we can't accept a contract that says: "I will only cut on myself once a week."

Once a contract is signed, you must help the juvenile be successful. If you see him slipping, remind him of the contract. Discuss his progress. Meet with him and review the contract at the end of the contract period. Then make a new contract. This practice will reinforce the steps of involvement and the contract.

And, it will help the juvenile see where he is in making choices that will undermine his own success.

Let's look at the scenario of Bryan and see a simple contract.

Bryan, 14-years-old, has been incarcerated for sexually molesting a five-year-old girl. The youth worker approached me after one of our training sessions.

Youth Worker:	"Mr. Jackson, you said you would talk with any kid we requested you to during our practicum training. Will you really do that?"
David:	"Yes, I will be happy to if you want me to."
Worker:	"Oh good. Maybe you can help me get this kid to change. He is driving us crazy."
David:	"I don't know about that, but I will be happy to show you how I would relate to him using Choice Theory. Remember there is nothing magical about it, but I find it has been helpful for me over the years. Who would you like me to see?"
Worker:	"His name is Bryan, and he just talks, talks, talks. He comes up to all of us and just wants to talk all the time. Jabber, jabber, jabber. He won't stop, and we have tried threatening and punishing and nothing works. I know you say those are the deadly habits, but when a kid won't mind you, what are you going to do? We are desperate."

Bryan walked into the room and looked at me. The youth worker introduced him to me. He just nodded and when I offered my hand, he shook it limply. We both sat down, and I smiled at him.

David: "Has anyone told you why you are here and who I am?"

Bryan shook his head and said nothing. The behavior was contrary to what had been described to me.

David: "If it is O.K. with you, I'd just like to get to know you. Is that all right with you?"

Bryan: "Yes."

David: "Where is your home, Bryan? May I call you by your first name?"

Bryan: Bryan grinned at me. "Yeah. That's what it is."

David: "Will you call me David?"

Bryan: "If you want me to."

David: "Great. Where is your home?"

Bryan: "Muncie."

David: "If you were there right now, and wanted to do anything you wanted, what would you be doing?"

Bryan: Bryan cocked his head from side to side, and then he took a big breath. "I would go to the mall and play video games."

David: "You like video games best of anything?"

Bryan: "Yeah, except eating. I like to eat hamburgers, but you never get them in here. Just beets, potatoes, more beets and a bunch of other vegetables. But I like hamburgers. I'd have hamburgers for breakfast if I could. Am I talking too much again? The counselors tell me I should shut up, that I talk too much."

David: "Which do you like most, hamburgers or talking?"

Bryan: "I like both."

David: "Isn't it hard to talk with a mouth full of three hamburgers?"

Bryan:	"Three?" He looked hard at me, then grinned.
	"You're putting me on aren't you?"
David:	"Yeah, is that O.K.?"

Bryan nodded.

David:	"Now Bryan, tell me something. What is the reason you think the counselors wanted you and me to talk?"
Bryan:	"They think you can make me quit talking so much."
David:	"Hey Bryan, we got a secret don't we?"

He looked at me quizzically, but he said nothing. I remained quiet. Several seconds went by before Bryan said anything.

Bryan:	"What is the secret?"
David:	"You and I know that I can't make you do anything you don't want to do, right?"
Bryan:	"Huh?"
David:	"It makes sense doesn't it Bryan? Can you make anybody do anything if they really don't want to?"
Bryan:	"No."
David:	"O.K. Can anybody really make you or me do anything we don't want to?"
Bryan:	"No, I guess not."
David:	"So, let's talk about the talking. Do you think it is something you would rather not do so much of, or would you like for things to just go on the way they are and have everybody yelling at you?"
Bryan:	"No, I would like to stop, but I just can't. I don't know why, I just can't."

David:	"If I could help you find something different to do, would you be interested?"
Bryan:	"Sure, but I don't know what it is. I want to talk about my problems all the time, and the counselors and other staff really get pissed. You don't know what it's like, and I can't stop just because they yell and try to make me stop. There, see I'm doing it now, and I don't even think about it."
David:	"It's O.K. In fact, Bryan, I have my watch, and I would like for you to go on talking about your problems to me right now for five minutes. O.K.?"

I am using a paradoxical technique described by Dr. Robert Wubbolding, author of *Reality Therapy into the 21st Century*. You are asking the client to make things better by making them worse. I would caution not to use this technique with pyromaniacs and other violent behaviors.

Bryan:	"But, that's different. I can't think of enough to say for that long."
David:	"Hey, that was only five seconds. Come on. For five minutes, are you ready?"
Bryan:	"You are tricking me. I can't think of anything to say. How did you do that?"
David:	"Bryan, you chose not to talk. Did I put my hand over your mouth?"
Bryan:	"No. But what do you mean I chose not to talk?"
David:	"Did I put my hand over your mouth?"
Bryan:	"No."
David:	"So. Who controlled whether you chose to talk or not?"
Bryan:	"I guess I did, but you made it so hard."
David:	"What were you thinking when I asked you to talk?"
Bryan:	"It was weird. The thought of church came to my mind."
David:	"What do you mean?"

Bryan:	"That word just came to my mind. I don't know why. What do you think it means?"
David:	"I think you may have just come up with a way to make better choices."
Bryan:	"Huh?"
David:	"Bryan, would you really like to talk less?"
Bryan:	"Yes, I would. I really get a lot of hassle when I talk too much."
David:	"Would you be willing to think of something else when you choose to talk too much?"
Bryan:	"Yeah, but what?"
David:	"Well, what word came into your mind that you think helped you?"
Bryan:	"Church?"
David:	"It's worth a try. What do you say? When you find yourself choosing to get yourself into trouble with your mouth what are you going to think?"
Bryan:	"Church. Church. Yeah, I can do that. That's kind of weird. Do I have to say it out loud?"
David:	"No, just think it. Now I have another suggestion, are you ready for it?"
Bryan:	"What?"
David:	"Ask your teachers and counselors, and all those people you talk a lot at, to just say 'church'to you when you start talking so much. That will help remind you to think church. Are you willing to do that?"
Bryan:	"I'm willing to try that."
David:	"Bryan, when will you tell them about your word?"
Bryan:	"Tomorrow, I'll do it tomorrow."
David:	"How about today?"
Bryan:	"Well, I could tell my counselor over there and my teacher this afternoon."

David:	"Bryan, I think you have come up with a good plan. But tell me, how might you sabotage this plan?"
Bryan:	"What does that mean?"
David:	"It means how might you destroy your plan?"
Bryan:	"By not doing it?"
David:	"Yeah. Are you going to sabotage it by not doing it?"
Bryan:	"No."
David:	"Bryan, how can I know that you told your counselor over there?"
Bryan:	Bryan turned to his counselor and grinned. "I'll tell her right now, and you can hear me."
David:	"Sounds like a winner to me. Go ahead."
Bryan:	Bryan turned in his chair. "If I start talking like you don't want me to, and I forget to think my magic word, will you say it to me?"
Worker:	"Sure Bryan. What is the magic word again?"
Bryan:	"Oh yeah. It is church."
David:	I looked at Bryan as he turned back to me in his chair. "Bryan, I am very pleased to have met you, and I am proud of the way you have worked here today. How about another handshake?"

This time, there was some firmness in Bryan's handshake.

I returned to conduct some follow up training six weeks later, and the counselor told me that Bryan's plan had worked for him. He was doing much better in the cottage and in his classes.

Summary

Having juveniles evaluate their behavior helps them to grow and change their behavior. You can help juveniles with their evaluation by asking judgment questions, such as "How will this help you?" These questions encourage juveniles to think about their behavior and how they can make better choices in the future.

Once they admit their behavior does not meet their needs, juveniles are ready to make better choices. At this point, your role is to help them work out a plan and make a contract.

Questions

1. Which of the following questions is a judgment question?

   _____ "What you did was inappropriate and downright rude. How do you expect me or anyone else to respond?"

   _____ "Will doing this help you stay out of trouble?"

   _____ "I keep telling you over and over and over. Why can't you do the right thing?"

2. List at least six traits of a good plan.

   • _____

   • _____

   • _____

   • _____

   • _____

   • _____

3. What question do you need to ask juveniles to move into the contract phase?

   _____

4. True/False. Once you make a contract with a juvenile, your work is done.

5. True/False. You should accept small increments of improvement in a juvenile's behavior.

 # Working with Groups

Objective

After reading this chapter, you will be able to:

- Define the acronym SAM
- Describe the importance of working with groups

Every day, in cottages, wards, group homes or units, we work with groups of juveniles. Choice Theory and Reality Therapy can and should be used with these groups. This chapter points out the value of this practice.

Step 11 of Involvement

Step 11, work in groups, is important because using peer group pressure and influence is a useful tool. A group of juveniles working with someone who did not fulfill his or her contract will refuse to accept excuses. In addition, the group will be harder on their peer than most adults. Your role in working with groups of juveniles, just as with individuals, is to connect and establish a trusting rela tionship. This role is true for all staff but even more so for line staff.

We will look first at a large group and a contract, then we will examine a smaller group with long range treatment goals and a contract.

Let's look now at the scenario involving a large group and a contract.

The SAM Plan

Several problems were occurring in a juvenile detention facility. There had been fights that were so serious that the city police were called to respond, and they had entered the facility with clubs drawn. One worker and two of the youth had to be transported to the emergency room for medical treatment because of the violent altercations.

Prior to this incident, a drive by shooting had occurred, and the kitchen windows of the facility had been shot out.

The last thing that was causing chaos involved the ceiling. The juveniles would hoist each other to the ceiling. Then, they would push the ceiling tiles up, crawl into the ceiling, and stay until they got hungry enough to come down. One staff member had fallen and broken his collarbone while trying to retrieve missing juveniles. The juveniles could roam around in the top of the two story facility. On two occasions, juveniles managed to get out onto the roof of the facility. Consequently, the maintenance crew bolted the roof doors shut, which took care of that problem.

I was asked to go into the center and do what I could to stop the problems. When asked by the judge what I would do to stop the problems, I answered, "I can't stop the youth any more than the police or your staff can stop the youth, but I will try to persuade them to stay out of the ceiling and stop their rumbles for a week. If that is successful, it will give your staff time to try some of the things I have been teaching them this week."

I did have something in my favor. I had been in the detention facility three different times during the week of the training I was conducting. During those visits, I had spent some time talking with the youth and asking about their lives. In other words, I had spent some time connecting with a few of the 110 boys and girls who were being detained pending court action in their cases. The facility had a capacity for 65 youth. This meant that many youth were sleeping on mattresses on the floor with three, four, and five in a cell.

I entered the detention dayroom where I met the superintendent who had been told I was coming.

Superintendent:	"The judge said you were coming to talk to the kids, so I got them all in the dayroom. We can put them up against the wall so you can talk."
David:	"That won't be necessary. I will just get out in the middle of the group and go from there."
Superintendent:	"Look. You go into the middle of that group, you are taking your life in your hands. You know we've had three big rumbles this week don't you?"
David:	"Yeah, I know, but it will be all right. I just want to talk to them."

There were large round tables and six to eight youth were sitting in chairs at the tables. There were eleven girls sitting toward the back at a table. They were segregated from the boys but within earshot of where I would be standing in the middle of the large room.

I walked between the tables, speaking to different youth as I went offering high fives now and then when I recognized some of the youth. I stopped right in the middle of the group and just stood there waiting for the noise to subside. In a few seconds, curiosity began to help the noise diminish. I just kept looking around and smiling while I waited. When the room became quiet enough, I said the following in a voice loud enough for all to hear.

David: "Guess what I heard? Oh, never mind, you could never guess in a million years."

I waited.

Youths: "Hey man, what kind of game is this? What you hear man? Come on tell us. He ain't heard nothin', he's just tryin' to chill us."

David: "I heard that someone in here wants a pizza party. Did I hear correct?"

Youths: "Yeah, man. Hey, that sound good. We don't want none of that shit that comes out of the kitchen."

David: "How about if it comes from Pizza Hut?"

Youths: "Yeah, Pizza Hut. That works (from the back). How about fried chicken? What we got to do. They gotta be a catch (from one of the girls). Do we get Cokes and Pepsis too?"

David: "Yeah, fried chicken, drinks and french fries. And yes, I want something from you. Now, is everybody interested? If not, just tell me and I'll be on my way."

A chorus of "yeas" and "yes, man" and other things that I could not make out, were shouted.

David: "Well, it sounded like everybody, but I really need to be sure. Is there anyone here who does not want such a party?"

One youth stood up and said, "If there is, he is gonna be everybody's enemy here."

David: "O.K. This deal is gonna be kinda like buying a house. The pizza party is the house. When you buy a house what do you have to do to get it?"

Youths: "Pay money. Steal it. Mortgage it." And other nonsensical comments.

David: "Can you get a house that is really your own if you don't pay somebody some money?"

Agreement was reached that you just don't get a house given to you.

David: "Well, since you guys and gals don't have the money to pay for this house, the pizza party, I would like to suggest you think of something else that would be worth money. Anybody have any ideas on what you could do while you are in here to sort of trade for the pizza party? It needs to be something that everyone will agree to work for it."

I waited for some time as they began to exchange ideas at the tables where they were seated. After about one minute, one youth toward the back of the group shouted out: "We could ask our friends to stop the drive by shootings."

David: "Hey! That sounds like a down payment on your house. Now there are extra costs, like closing costs and interest payments. What else would you be willing to do? Anyone? Speak up loud and clear."

After some more arguing amongst themselves, another youth said, "We could stop fighting and making the police come in after us."

David: "Wow! You guys must really want this house, your pizza party. I think you have almost bought it. What is one more thing you would be willing to do?"

No one said anything and a long time passed. A lot of "We don't know" could be heard. Finally, I gave the group a hint. I looked straight up at the ceiling tiles above me and said nothing. I continued to stare at the tiles until one youngster close to me shouted: "We could stay out of the ceiling!"

I slowly lowered my head until I was looking at the group. I slowly looked around the room before I spoke.

David: "What do you want on your pizza?"

There was a barrage of toppings yelled out, and I waited until things got quiet again.

David: "O.K. We have the payment for your house outlined. One, you're going to ask your friends to not drive by and shoot any more. Two, you're going to knock off the fighting, and three, you will stay out of the ceilings. That is great, but how long will you avoid fighting and stay out of the ceilings?"

There was a chorus of "forever," "one year," "six months" and "for an eternity." I waited until it was quiet. Then, I feigned surprise at the time factors.

David: "Oh my goodness. I would never ask you to stop fighting and stay out of the ceilings forever, or a year or even six months. C'mon people, get real. How long?"

The group suddenly got very quiet. I heard things like, "This dude's nuts," "What's he up to?" "What do we say now?" And "one month," "two months," and "three weeks." Again, I feigned surprise.

"Guys and gals get real with me. That's way too long."

One youth stood up and said: "Well man, you tell us. You think we wrong, tell us."

David: "O.K. Today is Wednesday, right? For your payment on the house, the pizza party, you have no fights and no ceiling stuff the rest of today, tomorrow, and Friday. Then, on Saturday we have the pizza part. O.K.?"

There were lots of comments about how good the deal was and assurances that the youth could carry it out. They can only control their behavior—not the behavior of those outside. But they did get the word to friends outside to "cool it."

The plan I worked with the youth is called a SAM plan and was designed by Dr. Robert Wubbolding, Director of Training for the William Glasser Institute.

SAM is the acronym for the plan:

S is for simple. Make the plan simple and easily recognizable. The boys were to stop fighting and stay out of the ceilings, a very simple plan.

A is for attainable. The plan is easily attainable. Avoiding fighting and stay ing out of the ceilings are easily attainable.

M is for measurable. Avoiding fighting and staying out of the ceilings are easily measurable.

The time frame for SAM is designed to ensure success. Any unreasonable time frame such as one month, two months, a year, and so forth ensures failure. The small success of a SAM plan gives staff an opportunity to build upon that suc cess and plan for more successful plans.

David: "O.K. We have a contract, but like all good contracts, we must write it down on paper and all of us sign it. If anyone breaks the contract, we will have to start all over and build another contract. No pizza this Saturday. We'll just work out another agreement and another date."

At this point, I got the superintendent to type up the contract and run copies. Each table got a copy, and each boy and girl read the contract, then signed it. All of the youth signed the contract.

Saturday came with no further incidents, and the pizza party was a great success. The detention workers began using negotiating and compromising. But more important, they began making successful efforts and being more friendly and connecting with the youth. Three more months went by before another incident of fighting occurred, and the staff were able to defuse it without having to call the police. No more ceiling incidents occurred, and the drive by shootings stopped.

Another scenario in working with groups to develop a contract is the CHILL OUT Program that is covered in the following scenario.

CHILL OUT—Fourteen Delinquents in a Maximum Security Cottage

I was invited into a maximum security cottage to work with 14 delinquents, ages 14 to 17. They were in detention pending their adjudication and sentencing hearings.

The staff were having some problems with the youth. There had been four attempts to escape over the 15 foot high fence with razor wire on the top. There was great concern that the youth would be seriously injured if they could not be persuaded to stop the attempts. There was also concern for the public if some of the more violent youngsters escaped back into the community. In addition, there were fights occurring between youth, and between youth and staff.

Four of the delinquents were African American: Kareem, Richard, Raschad, and Omar. Six youth were Caucasian: Robert, Frank, Timmy, Brandon, Phil and Derrick. Four youth were Hispanic: Garcia, Manny, Mario and Pablo. The alleged offenses ranged from breaking and entering to assault and murder. All had some contact with drugs, either dealing or using. The popular drug was cocaine followed closely by marijuana.

I had four goals as I began this project. To be successful, I must develop TRUST between all the youth and me. Trust is a two way street. To accomplish this, I must make the first goal a priority or there is no possible way of successfully achieving the remaining three goals; however, the work of having a friend continues on and is included in each of the three remaining goals.

1. Connect with the youth and become a friend—the right hand of trust.
2. Use external controls only in an emergency. I know that connecting is extremely important. Without any connecting, the project is doomed. To help me eliminate the use of external controls, I must not use the deadly habits.
3. Teach the youth Choice Theory, which is the opposite of external control psychology.
4. Conduct social skills training, using Glasser's Choice Theory and Lead Management, and do so within the framework of social skills training as described by Arnold Goldstein (Goldstein, *Skillstreaming the Adolescent*).

I spent two days in the cottage just connecting with the 14 youth, which was not an easy task. No one paid much attention to me the first morning, but by the afternoon, I began to hear the youth talking with each other.

I heard things such as:

- "Who is this dude?"
- "Is he some kind of spy for de judge?"
- "I'll bet he's a cop."

Finally, on the second morning, one of the youngsters asked me:

Youth: "Hey man, who the hell are you? You come in here and don't say nothing. Just smiling and playing checkers and games with some of us and just visitin' and doing that stupid magic trick. How the hell you make that thing disappear? What's the deal?"

Everyone stopped talking, and the youth watched me to see what I was going to say or do.

David: "Well, I'm just a dude who would like to try and make it better for you guys while you are in here. Is that something you would be interested in hearing about?"

I looked at each of the 14 youth while I spoke. A couple yawned. One spit on the floor, receiving a verbal reprimand from one of the youth workers present. But the rest started looking at me and listening. There was a chorus of comments and questions. I waited until things got quiet.

David: "I have a proposition to put to you guys. It is called Chill Out. If you want to know more about the proposition, I'll tell you. What do you say?"

By now, most all the boys were curious, and several indicated they wanted to know more.

David: "I'll talk with each one of you separately and see if you want to participate in Chill Out. If you do, fine. If you don't, that is fine also. It is your choice. Now who would like to meet with me first?"

| Kareem: | Kareem grunted. "I ain't goin' to no Chill Out shit." |

No one said anything for a few seconds. Then Robert spoke.

| Robert: | "What is this Chill Out you talking about?" |
| David: | "Well Robert, that is part of what I will explain to each of you as we meet, if you choose to meet with me. O.K.?" |

Again they were quiet. Then Kareem spoke.

| Kareem: | "I'll go first, just to see what this crap is." |

The others followed almost in unison. I had prepared little pieces of paper with numbers one through 14. I pulled out number one, folded the rest of the num bers, and placed them in one of the boy's caps. I asked each of the boys to reach into the cap and choose a piece of paper. I told them that would be the order in which I would interview each of them.

The objective is to expose the youth to a number of moral dilemmas. They con sequently discuss and reason at different levels of moral thinking. I am inten tionally creating cognitive conflict so that the resolution will advance their moral reasoning to a higher level than they have been exposed. This practice is based upon the findings of Lawrence Kohlberg (Kohlberg, *The Philosophy of Moral Development*). To use moral reasoning by itself, however, will be inef fective. I must make friends and establish trust before the youth will internalize:

- the relationships that we are forming, and
- the Choice Theory ideas and social skills that they are learning.

I give the youth every opportunity to choose, and I use the word frequently. This point is the beginning of teaching them Choice Theory.

I met with each of the 14 juveniles separately, but we will review only the first individual contract session.

David: "Come on Kareem, if you are ready?"
Kareem: "No problem."
David: Kareem immediately sat down in the chair closest to the door. "Hey man, I don't bite. Get up here by the table so you can read this contract and ask me anything you want to. O.K.?"

Kareem grumbled something about he'd hit me in the mouth if I tried to bite him, and he moved his chair up to the small table.

David: "What would you like to know first?"
Kareem: He stared at me, scratched his head, and leaned back in his chair. "What the hell is CHILL OUT?"

I held up the tee shirt for him to see, as I did for each of the following youth I interviewed.

David: "The letters stand for Choices Involved in Learning to Live. The OUT is from Martin Luther King. Overcome, Understand and Trust."
Kareem: "Is that what Martin Luther King said?"
David: "That was part of what he said when he was telling us all that we should be each other's friend. Do you like Martin Luther King?"
Kareem: "Of course, man. He fought for our rights."
David: "Then, do you think his ideas are good?"
Kareem: "Of course man. He was real smart and helped us out a lot."
David: "Well, when he said we should all be brothers and sisters and friends, does that make sense?"
Kareem: "Yeah, but none of the whites wants to do that."

David:	"That's why I'm here. I want to do that. Will you help me?"
Kareem:	"What do I have to do in return?"
David:	"Let's read the CHILL OUT contract. That will explain a lot."

We read the contract and Kareem had some questions about not fighting if he was picked on, or called names, or his mama was called names.

David:	"If you will let me, I will help you deal with stuff like that. Will you let me?"
Kareem:	"I don't know man. I've got to think about all this shit. This is heavy crap man."
David:	"That's O.K. Take your time. What do you think about the contract? Do you want to be the first one, or do you want to wait and see if anyone else is going to sign it before you do?"
Kareem:	"If I sign it and don't like it, can I quit anytime?"
David:	"I ask you to talk to me first if there is a problem, and see if we can work it out . Would you agree to that?"
Kareem:	"Yeah, O.K. man. I'll do it. Can I have my tee shirt first?"
David:	"Sure."
Kareem:	Kareem slipped the tee shirt on. "Where do I sign?"

We both signed, and I told him I would make him a copy he could keep. He seemed pleased with the idea of having his own copy. When we left the office, he was strutting out into the dayroom where all the other boys could see him in his tee shirt. He was very puffed up and turned around several times.

Kareem:	When several youth asked what happened, he said: "You'll see, you'll see."

The rest of the boys were interviewed. They signed their copy of the contract and received their tee shirt. The following is the contract that was presented to each of the youth.

CONTRACT, AN AGREEMENT BETWEEN (the boy's name and mine).

CHILL OUT PROGRAM—(Choices Involved in Learning to Live—Overcome, Understand, and Trust)

Party of the FIRST PART—(JUVENILE'S NAME).

Party of the second part—(DAVID JACKSON)

At this point, I discussed with each youth what these terms meant. The term "first part" is by the juvenile's name on purpose. I will do everything I can to help each youth satisfy his power need. Juvenile offenders often meet their power need through disruptive behavior. Anything I can do to help them meet their need in acceptable ways will be helpful and bring us closer together. I even capitalize the first part and use lower case for the second part.

THIS IS MY WORD: I (JUVENILE'S NAME), THE FIRST PART, agree to take part in learning about my choices and other skills to make my life better and free of legal consequences during this CHILL OUT program.

Notice the use of "THIS IS MY WORD." Regardless of the crimes youth have committed, their word is important to them.

I will do this without fighting, trying to escape, or exhibiting other behavior that might hurt my chances for freedom. In return, I will receive certain things, as outlined below, from David Jackson. I give my word in this contract.

This is my word: I, David Jackson, the second part, agree to do everything possible, within the laws and rules of the court, to make things better for (JUVENILE'S NAME), THE FIRST PART. David Jackson will ask what is wanted from (JUVENILE'S NAME) and the other occupants of this cottage, and, working together as a team, WE WILL find the best way to get these wants to the Juvenile Judge for his consideration. In addition, David Jackson will provide a CHILL OUT tee shirt, free, to (JUVENILE'S NAME) and his colleagues. I give my word in this contract.

I spent a great deal of time with each of the juveniles explaining this agreement and what certain words meant, including colleagues.

IN PARTNERSHIP, WE AGREE TO THE ABOVE:

Signed By:

THE FIRST PART—(Juvenile's signature).

The second part—(my signature).

Date_____.

All 14 boys chose to take part and signed the contract. I kept the original and made a copy for each of them.

As I talked with the boys, each discussion was a little bit different because of the personality of each youth and how we were connecting.

When all 14 boys had signed their contract and received their tee shirts, I returned to the dayroom. I sat down in one of the easy chairs and observed the interaction going on between the youth. There was some pinching the material of each other's shirts and comments such as:

- "Hey; your shirt ain't as smooth as mine."
- "Mine is made of silk man. Pure silk. Ya'll eat cher' hearts out. Mine is real silk."

Finally, Robert looked at me, and he pointed at me to the others.

Robert: "Hey look. He's just sittin' there watchin' us. I tell you he's got to be a spy for the judge."

Everyone laughed at Robert.

Mario: Then Mario looked at me. "I think he is a good amigo. I may like him a little bit, but we shall see."

Giving them some space to process what had just transpired is important. This processing is part of connecting as a team to try and make things better. When they were ready, they returned their attention to me.

David: "Well, I'm glad somebody may like me a little bit. I've worked my butt off trying to convince you guys that I really want to help you make things better. I can't do it myself, but together, I think we can make it a little better. Are you ready to begin?"

Everyone got to their feet and several asked what we were going to do.

David: "Let's all sit down, and I'll tell you what I want you to start out doing. I want to find out what you guys want that would make your stay here better. Not 100 percent all right, but better."

Several of the boys asked how I was going to find out what would make things better.

David: "There are 14 of you guys, so I would like for you to count off by one, two, three, and four, then start at one again. You know, starting here with you Omar, you will be a number one. Now, Pablo call out your number."

Pablo: "TWO!"

The boys counted off until all had called out their number. We had three groups. One had four in it, and the other two had five in them. I gave each group a piece of flip chart paper and a black marker.

David: "O.K. guys. Decide on a name for your group, and print it at the top of the paper. Then I want you to write down some things you want out of this contract. Let's start with four or five things."

The purpose of this effort is to encourage them to focus on the task and not just start writing. These instructions help them to think about their choices.

David: "Take your time and talk it over with each other in your group. One of you act as the person who prints the want list. Any questions? O.K. You can go anywhere in the dayroom you choose. Go to it."

I listened as the youth discussed, argued and cajoled each other, as they came up with a list of wants. The youth took 25 minutes to finish the task. Most of them had more than five wants and had to make some compromises to get down to the requested number. This exercise is specifically designed to require some negotiation and compromise, which exposes the youth to these social skills.

When they were finished, I gave them some masking tape and asked them to tape their lists to the wall. When all lists were taped, I asked them to select a pre senter and read the lists off to us, and we would then discuss each list. The lists consisted of some very unrealistic items. One such item was the want of a rifle range between the 15 foot fence and the front door of the cottage. I did not laugh, criticize or use any of the other deadly habits that destroy relationships. I was aware that I wanted to say things that would bring us closer together and not drive us farther apart. So I asked a value question.

David: "Hey, a rifle range. Is that something you think the judge will consider?"

The group quickly marked through that want. The other groups reviewed their lists and marked through some of the more outlandish wants.

Another such want was a pet pony they could ride around the outside of the cottage.

We examined all the wants, and finally there were four wants that everyone agreed upon.

1. Be allowed to swim once a week. The boys could look out the dayroom window and see the members of the open cottages walking in their swim suits to the outdoor swimming pool every afternoon. The pool was about 100 yards from their cottage. We were in the middle of July, and they could see the water splash up as the other juveniles dove into the pool time and again.
2. Be allowed to eat in the dining hall once a week. Currently, the meals were brought in on hot food trays, three times a day.
3. Be allowed to go to town and attend a movie once a month.
4. Go bowling downtown once a week.

Kareem: Kareem looked at all the lists and then stood up.
           "When are you going to ask the judge for all this stuff?"
David: "Hey man. They are not my lists. They are your lists. I'll help you figure out how you want to present them, but I'm not the man that is going to do that."

Kareem:	"Now how in the hell can we see the judge to ask him for this stuff?"
David:	"Well, I'll get you an appointment if that is how you want to do it. But, I would not recommend that all 14 of you ask to see the judge at the same time for four things you want. You need some of you to represent the others. Do you think that would be a good idea?"
Kareem:	"Yeah, yeah, but how are we going to do that?"
David:	"Well, I have a suggestion, if anyone is interested?"

A chorus of "yes mans" echoed through the room.

David:	"I suggest you elect three senators to present your requests to the judge."

When several of the boys asked what a senator was, I explained it to them, along with the election process. I asked how many would like to run for one of the three positions.

All 14 boys decided to run for senator. They wanted me to help set up the election.

David:	"Every one of you needs to prepare a political speech outlining why everyone should vote for you. Like, you will explain how you will present the wants to the judge. No threats or violence are allowed of course because that would be against the cottage rules. Right?" When no one answered I repeated, "Right?"

There were several O.K.s and yeahs. "So, what do we need to do?"

David: "You will be allowed 30 seconds to one minute to make your political speech. We will have little pieces of paper for each of you to write your votes down. I say votes, because each of you will have two votes, and I want you to write them down on the same piece of paper. You cannot vote for the same person both times. Each vote must have a separate name, or your vote will be invalid."

I explained this procedure until the youth indicated they understood. Then we had the speeches. At the end of the speeches, we had the votes. Everyone got at least one vote, which was expected, because each of the boys voted for himself. When the rest of the votes were counted, the winners were Kareem, Phil and Raschad.

I asked the boys to think about what they might say to the judge in their presentation of the four wants. Then we would role play it to see how their presentations would look.

The next day, we role played the scenario of presenting the wants to the judge. Finally, after a some frustration, the youth decided how they were going to do it, and did a good job of role playing.

I had arranged a meeting with the judge, and the next day, the youth were taken to court and presented their wants to the judge. They had wanted me to go with them, but I declined, encouraging them to do it themselves. The judge decided they should be allowed to swim every day, not just once a week. They would be allowed to eat in the dining hall once every week. There would be neither movies nor bowling in town.

The senators were elated, and reported back to their constituents. They were anything but humble as they explained how they had talked with the judge and gotten most of what they had wanted.

The next day, we started Choice Theory training, which lasted three days. Then we began a full two weeks of social skills training. The social skills training steps included:

- Modeling
- Role playing
- Performance feedback
- Transfer and maintenance of training.

The social skills included:

1. Beginning Social Skills (eight skills)—listening, asking a question, and saying thank you are a few of these skills.
2. Advanced Social Skills (six skills)—asking for help, joining in, and apol ogizing are a few of these skills.
3. Skills for dealing with feelings (seven skills)—knowing your feelings, and dealing with someone else's anger are a few of these skills.
4. Empathy training (includes a mask exercise)—understanding the feelings of others, and doing a paper mache imprint of each of juvenile's face (the mask exercise)—so that each one can explain what he sees of himself.
5. Skills for dealing positively with aggression (nine skills)—negotiating, using self control, and standing up for your rights without fighting are a few of these skills.
6. Skills for defusing anger (four skills)—learning techniques to avoid or deal with angry feelings are some of these skills.
7. Skills for dealing with stress (eleven skills)—making a complaint, answering a complaint, responding to failure, and dealing with an accusa tion are a few of these skills.
8. Planning Skills (seven skills)—deciding on something to do, setting a goal, making a decision, and concentrating on a task are a few of these skills (Goldstein, *Skillstreaming the Adolescent*).

All the youth eventually were adjudicated. Six were committed to the custody of the state juvenile department and placed into state operated institutions. One was found accountable as an adult and received time in an adult prison. Two were placed into open treatment cottages operated by the county, and five were placed on probation for an indeterminate period of time.

The follow up five years later revealed: one was still in adult prison; one was killed in a drive by shooting; two were referred for further violation as an adult; two had their probation rescinded and were committed to state institutions; and the remaining eight had no record of further delinquent or criminal referrals.

Summary

Working with groups is important because peer influence is helpful in encouraging juveniles to fulfill their behavioral contracts. Peer groups usually accept no excuses and are harder on peers than most adults. Your role in working with groups is the same as working with individuals—connect and build a relationship. The SAM plan, developed by Dr. Robert Wubbolding, and the Chill Out Program are useful tools in group work.

Questions

1. Define the acronym SAM.

_____

_____

_____

2. What is the purpose of the Chill Out Program?

_____

_____

3. True/False. The Chill Out Program requires juveniles to work as a team.

4. True/False. External controls should be used only in an emergency. To avoid using external controls in nonemergency situations, you must avoid using the deadly habits.

5. List five social skills that juveniles need to learn and master.

- _____

- _____

- _____

- _____

- _____

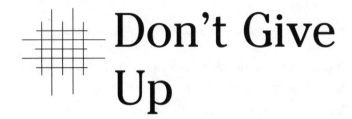 # Don't Give Up

Objectives

After reading this chapter, you will be able to:

- Explain P-A-R-T
- Describe how to help juveniles stop crying and continue talking about the topic that made them cry
- Explain why we should never give up

In this chapter, we will discuss the last two steps of involvement:

- Step 12: P-A-R-T (giving praise, approval, reward and touch), and
- Step 13: Don't Give Up.

Step 12 of Involvement

Step 12: **P-A-R-T** is critical. We all want and seek praise, approval, reward, and touch. The juveniles in your care, custody and control have been lectured by the best. What they have not gotten is praised for doing a good job. They have not received approval from those they love and respect. They have not been rewarded for a job well done. And, the touch they have received may have been the back of someone's hand. Let juveniles know when they do well. If you can reward their positive behavior with a special privilege, so much the better.

Rewarding with a special privilege serves two purposes:

- It gives the juveniles some special privilege that they have earned, which helps them meet their need for power.
- It serves as a model for the other juveniles.

Praise and approval go hand in hand. It takes precious little of our time to say statements such as: "I really appreciate the way you talked in group today. You were right on with your comments." "The dayroom really looks good today, and I know you were on the cleaning detail."

Some professionals believe that comments on what was done are best. For example, you might say, "Wow, look at that floor and the way it shines." This comment lets the juvenile make the connection that he or she is responsible for the way the floor shines. Sometimes, it may be better to be more direct. For example, you might say, "Jose, look at that floor and the way it shines. You really put a lot of work into that, and it shows." Another example of a direct statement is: "Sherry, thanks for sharing your grade on that homework. Wow, a B! That is great, and I am so proud of you. I remember when you thought that was impossible, and now you are getting A's and B's on a regular basis. Your plans are really working out because you are working on your plan."

Sometimes, we hear from careworkers who say, "Why should we compliment juveniles for doing what they are supposed to do? They are supposed to keep their areas clean, make their beds, and hang up their clothes. They are supposed to stay out of trouble. They are supposed to go to school, and the school here is so easy, they should be making A's all the time."

The answer is simple. These same workers are supposed to: come to work and arrive on time; provide quality care for youth; prevent escapes and fights; and protect the juveniles from themselves and others. Yet, each of these workers enjoys the compliments and warm feelings evoked when someone notices their efforts and praises them. A part of love and belonging is recognition from someone else that we are people of value and make contributions. We all enjoy being appreciated for our contributions and for being ourselves.

A few words of caution on touch: not all touch is appropriate. Touch can be mis-interpreted, and not all people like to be touched. Be aware of these points, and also be aware of your facilitiy's policies and procedures. Do not do anything that is contrary to the policies and procedures. When we talk of touch, we are talking about shaking hands, a pat on the back, or a brush touch on the arm. We are also talking about eye-to-eye contact.

In his research, Dr. James Garbarino tells us that most kids who kill have dam-aged souls, unable to connect with love to the world around them. Or, perhaps some combination of temperament and early experience has sent them looking for love in all the wrong places. Human development proceeds from attachment in the first year of life. Starting at about three months of age, babies come to know and love the people who care for them. By the age of nine months, most babies have formed a specific attachment to one or more caregivers. This attachment is a mixture of knowing them in their particularity and feeling for them, as special individuals, a special sense of positive *CONNECTION*. In the absence of this "object" of their attachment, babies become wary and with-drawn, defensive and captured by their anxiety. (Garbarino, *Lost Boys—Why Our Sons Turn Violent and How We Can Save Them*)

Garbarino points out that after the concept of attachment was accepted as a cen-tral theme in the study of child development, psychologists began exploring varieties of attachment. They came to focus on four forms: secure, insecure-avoidant, insecure-ambivalent, and disorganized-disoriented.

We would include many other delinquents, not just those who kill, as having difficulty or being unable to connect with love to the world around them. Many delinquents fall under the latter three forms of attachment. That is why it is difficult to be a friend to these youngsters. It takes patience and a will on the counselor's or careworker's part to NOT GIVE UP! We saw this in Chapter 8 with Donnie who took 20 seconds to answer questions put to him. It was patience and not giving up that enabled the counselor to be successful.

In the same chapter, we saw Leroy choosing suspicious behavior of the counselor in an effort to avoid connecting. The counselor rolls his chair closer to Leroy while simultaneously stating a desire to be friends with the young man. So, we see the counselor not only stating the desire to be friends or to be friendlier but also moving physically closer to Leroy. The counselor uses humor to help penetrate that suspicious shroud which Leroy wears for his emotional protection. And in the scenario with Jesse, we see the counselor stating that he does not like delinquent behavior but—despite not knowing the boy long—he cares about what happens to Jesse. When Jesse rejects the idea of the counselor caring, the counselor, David, steers the conversation to a topic they both have in common, grandmas. As a result, the connection is nurtured. If David had used external control, doing so would have destroyed any possibility of a positive relationship developing. The hard work at connecting finally pays off when Jesse shows his acceptance by asking if David will assign the case to himself. Jesse says, "Hell, you aren't such a bad dude. I'll go with you."

In the next scenario in this chapter, we will see the probation officer working with Marilynn. When she chooses depressing and begins crying, he walks around the desk and puts a supporting hand on her shoulder. When she asks for a hug, he summons the secretary to his office, and together they provide the requested hug. At the end of the session, David rewards Marilynn by saying, "Marilynn, I'm proud of you. You really worked hard today." At the next session, when Marilynn shows him her grade card, he comments, "That's great! Wow! You must be extremely proud!"

Step 13 of Involvement

The last step of involvement is **DON'T GIVE UP!!!** The juveniles in your care, control and custody have had a lifetime of inappropriate and irresponsible behavior. You cannot help them change overnight—but you can help them change. Be an agent of change.

To illustrate this point, we will use three actual scenarios: one involving David, one involving Larry, and one involving Bill Glasser. First, we will review the scenario involving David.

Marilynn

Marilynn, 16-years-old, was arrested for solicitation along with her brother Dennis, age ten.

Six months ago, they were referred for bicycle theft and released to their parents with a warning from the intake officer. Marilynn also has a history of truancy since the sixth grade, but she has never been held back.

A vice squad officer in the red light district arrested Marilynn when he was approached by her and propositioned for money. She promised the officer if he let her go, she would "grant him some favors free of charge."

I was the assigned probation officer after Marilynn had been adjudicated as a delinquent. I met her for the first time when she was brought to my office by my supervisor.

Supervisor: "Marilynn, this is Mr. Jackson. He will be your probation officer. Mr. Jackson, this is Marilynn."

David: "Hi Marilynn, would you like to have a seat? Any chair that you choose will be fine."

Marilynn just nodded, and she kept standing.

David:	"Well, you seemed to have made it through your court experience in one piece, but it can be pretty scary."
Marilynn:	"Are you kidding? This shit doesn't scare me. I'm not a little kid."
David:	"You don't have to be a little kid to be scared of something, wouldn't you agree?"
Marilynn:	"Naw. It don't matter. Say, how long are you going to keep me in here today?"
David:	"Do you have something else to do that is important to you?"
Marilynn:	"Yeah. Something that is always more important than just chattering. You know what I mean."

Marilynn didn't take long to choose a provocative pattern of behavior that she would continue to use in our sessions for a some time.

David:	"Why don't you tell me what you mean, maybe I'll under stand you a little better. I think it is important that we both understand each other so we can work together."
Marilynn:	"If you don't know, I can't tell you. But let's work together. I like that ... working together."
David:	"Marilynn, what does working together mean to you?"
Marilynn:	"Man, you are really the straight arrow aren't you? I mean working together. You know. Getting it on. Now you surely get my meaning. If you don't, maybe I should trade you in for another probation officer."
David:	"That would be fine, if you are going have trouble talking with me. I'm sure Mrs. Teagarden or the judge might even work personally with you."
Marilynn:	"WHOA! Take it easy Jackson. I'm not complaining, I'm just trying to add a little spice to this deal we got going here."
David:	"Isn't that little spice that you choose, as you call it, what put you in detention and then to court?"

Marilynn:	"You could say that."
David:	"What do you say?"
Marilynn:	"Oh man, this is going to be a drag, I can see that right from the start."
David:	"Well, Marilynn, probation is always a drag. I've never had a young person your age come in here and say, 'Golly, David, I'm really glad to be here on probation. I really appreciate what you are doing for me, and I hope you never take me off probation.' I've never heard that, but I'm still waiting."

Marilynn stared at me. She slowly shook her head, and finally sat down in the chair next to my desk.

Marilynn:	"This isn't exactly what I expected. This is the pits."
David:	"Look Marilynn, I want to be your friend. I don't think you have ever had an adult friend."

Marilynn leaned over and started laughing. She laughed deep guffaws for several seconds.

Marilynn:	"Oh buster. You don't have any idea how many men friends I have had."
David:	"Well, it is obvious that your idea of friend and my idea of friend are two completely different ideas."

Marilynn batted her eyes at me and rolled a shoulder.

Marilynn:	"Well, buster, would you like to know my definition of a friend?"
David:	"Marilynn, I think I already know your definition."
Marilynn:	"Oh? Tell me."

David: "Look Marilynn, if we waste time talking about your idea of getting into the sack with some dude being the definition of a friend, do you think you will be getting off probation sooner or later?"

Marilynn: "If I tell you all about my friendly times, it may help you get off, and if you get off, you can do me the favor of letting me off probation."

David: "Marilynn, it just doesn't work that way. Now do you want to know my definition of a friend?"

Marilynn: "Do I have to?"

David: "Nope, you sure don't. It is your choice. The only thing you have to do has been written in the court's decision, and that is that you report every week to me, stay in school and continue passing, and no more of the propositioning crap. Now it really is all up to you. You can choose to violate any of those probation rules set out by the judge and if you do, where did he say he would send you?"

Marilynn: Marilynn became very quiet and sat up straight as she thought about what I had said. "He said he would send me to the girls' training school."

David: "Is that what you want to see happen?"

Marilynn: "No, shithead, of course not. Do I look stupid?"

David: "No, contrary to that, you appear to be a very bright young lady. My guess is that you are quite intelligent."

Marilynn: "Oh, don't give me that crap. You know I have a high I.Q. because you read the psychologist's report on me. Haven't you?"

David: "No I haven't. It probably is in your social history, and I don't read those things."

Marilynn: "You are one hell-uv-a probation officer. You don't even care enough to read about me."

David: "All I'm interested in Marilynn is the here and now. Whatever you've done in the past or has happened to you in the past is

	done, and we can't undo it, so why waste our time there? I'll listen to a little if you just have to go there, but I can guarantee it will not shorten your probation stay, and might even take up valuable time that would shorten it. So kiddo, it's your choice."
Marilynn:	"O.K. O.K. You've made your point. And what's this shit you keep saying about choice."
David:	"Well, Marilynn, I believe that everything we do that has a purpose are choices we make."
Marilynn:	"How about sneezing?"
David:	"Remember? I said anything that has purpose in our lives. All this stuff you have done in the office was a choice by you, and everything I have done is my choice. That's not too hard to understand is it?"
Marilynn:	"Yeah, but wait a minute. I went to a counselor when I was in the eighth grade, and he wanted to know all about how my mother treated me, and my father's behavior with me. He said that we are products of our childhood."

Finally, Marilynn has gotten away from her provocative behavior for the time being. Being able to carry on a conversation on a different subject and give opinions and ask questions is a big part in the connecting process.

David:	"Marilynn, we may be a product of our past, but what we choose to do today with our lives is what is important. What do you choose to do with yours today?"
Marilynn:	"You're wrong! I didn't choose to come in here and see you. Ha. You're wrong. That guy made me come in here."
David:	"Oh? Did he drag you in here? No. You had a choice. If any of us are willing to put up with the consequences of what we choose, we can choose what we want."

Marilynn:	"No, he didn't drag me in here. But, if I hadn't come in here, he would have taken me right back into that courtroom, and I would have been gone to the slammer."
David:	"So, you chose to come in here rather than being sent to the slammer, is that not correct?"
Marilynn:	"O.K. So you made your point, but only a dummy would have 'chosen' to go to the slammer."
David:	"Great! Our time is about up, but we finally have established one very good thing here."

I waited and looked at her. She thought awhile before she said anything.

Marilynn:	"I'm waiting in immaculate constipation. What the hell good came out of this?"
David:	"We know that you are no dummy. See you next week, and I will be talking with your teachers this week to see if there is anything I can do to help my new friend. And when I say friend, it is my definition of friend."

Marilynn stared at me and started grinning.

Marilynn:	"You never did tell me your definition of what a friend is. So, what is it?"
David:	"Marilynn, I'm going to save that for next week, and I hope you don't stay up late at night worrying about it. In fact, I suspect you know what my definition is, but we will work on that thing next week. I like you Marilynn, but I don't care for the crap you chose that brought you here."

Second Session

Marilynn entered my office with a bounce. She smiled provocatively, sat down, and spread her legs.

Marilynn: "Well old probation officer of mine, here I am. Do me."

David: "Marilynn, I think you are overdone already, so let's get to work. Oh, I am glad to see you in spite of."

Marilynn: "What do you mean in spite of? What did I do?"

David: "Marilynn, I have to turn in a monthly report on all the juveniles I have on probation. I am having a difficult time writing something the judge might be pleased with. Bob and John are two of the three on probation who I am referring to. Who do you suppose the third one is?"

Marilynn: "Oh me oh my oh. I just couldn't start to guess. Does her name start with Marilynn?"

David: "My dear Marilynn, you must be psychic. Yep, all I have to write so far is that you are choosing to continue the kind of behavior that landed you here in the first place. Is that what you want me to report?"

For the first time, Marilynn chose to display her anger, to control depressing or other miserabling behaviors.

Marilynn: "You lousy son-of-a-bitch! You know if you give me a bad report that g***amn judge will yank me out of my home and stick me in some stupid girls' school."

David: "Not just any girls' school Marilynn, but one with bars on the windows, isn't that what the judge said in court?"

Marilynn: "Yes, yes, yes, but you said you wanted to be my friend. What kind of friend would turn in a report that would screw their friend?"

David: "That would be the kind of friend who would report what their friend had 'chosen' to do in the probation sessions. I repeat 'chosen' to do."

The room became very quiet before Marilynn spoke again.

Marilynn: "What would you do if I came around that desk and sat in your lap?"

David: "Marilynn, do you want to find a nice guy someday and start a family?"

Marilynn: "What the hell does that have to do with my sitting on your lap? God, what a nerd."

David: "Just answer the question. It relates to your question."

Marilynn: "Now how in the hell does that relate? But, yeah, someday, I'll have kids. So what?"

David: "O.K. What do you want to have? Boys? Girls? One of each? What? Come on bear with me, you'll see where this goes in a moment."

Marilynn: "All right smart-ass, I would like a boy and a girl. Now, are you satisfied?"

David: "O.K. Let's say you have a girl. Would you want her to come into a closed room and sit on an older man's lap?"

Marilynn glared at me.

Marilynn: "That's her business. She can do what she wants to. Isn't that right. That would be her choice."

Marilynn sneered as she spat out "choice."

David:	"Right? Yes, that's right, but that wasn't the question. The question is would YOU want your daughter to sit on a strange older man's lap?"
Marilynn:	"NO! And I'd beat the crap out of her if I caught her! There. Are you satisfied?"
David:	"And how could you teach your daughter not to choose that kind of behavior? Come on Marilynn, it is not a difficult question. What are you afraid of?"
Marilynn:	"D**n you!"

Marilynn slumped over in her chair, and I could see tears rolling down her cheeks.

People cry for a number of reasons: being joyful, being sad, to gain attention, to gain sympathy, and/or to avoid talking about something. To determine which one, you can use a simple technique. Ask the person if he or she wants to cry. If the person says "Yes," then allow him or her a few minutes to express that feeling. If the person says no—or I can't help it—tell the person to make eye-to-eye contact with you and maintain it. Make eye-to-eye contact and continue talking about the subject. In this case, it was not necessary. The tears will stop in about 30 seconds.

I got up and moved to her chair. I put my hand on her shoulder.

She looked up with her tear-stained face.

Marilyn:	"Will you give me a hug?"
David:	This situation is obviously difficult. "Yes, Marilynn, but it will have to be a supervised hug this time."

I called the secretary on the intercom, and she came to my office.

David:	"Stacy, Marilynn and I need a hug; will you help us with that?"
Stacy:	"Sure, what can I do?"
David:	"Stand up Marilynn, we are going to have a three-way hug."
Marilynn:	Marilynn stood up and started laughing through her tears. Then, as we hugged, she said: "This has got to be the craziest thing I've ever done."
David:	"Are you liking it?"
Marilynn:	"Yes, I guess so. It wasn't quite what I had in mind."
David:	"I know. But that's all part of growing up. How was it for you Stacy?"
Stacy:	"Different but nice. Need me anymore?"
David:	"Not for now and thanks Stacy, but keep your hugger handy, we never know with this kid."
Marilynn:	Marilynn smiled and thanked Stacy as she left the office. "You always got an answer, don't you?"
David:	"No, Marilynn, not always, but you and I can work better and better toward you making better choices in your life. I think you are really interested in doing that. Am I correct?"
Marilynn:	"Sometimes, I want to trust you, but it is hard. I've been me for so long, I don't know if I can change."
David:	"Look Marilynn, you choose to do the provocative things you do, isn't that right?"
Marilynn:	"Yeah, yeah, I know that, but I can't help it."
David:	Here is an opportunity to teach a little more Choice Theory to Marilynn. "Now, Marilynn, whose behaviors can you control?"
Marilynn:	"Well, I guess my own."
David:	"Can you control anyone else's but your own?"
Marilynn:	"No. You just proved that didn't you?"
David:	"And, can anyone else control your behavior?"
Marilyn:	"No. My parents try to, but they can't. The judge can."
David:	"Can the judge really control your behavior if you are willing

	to take whatever consequences there are for your choices?"
Marilynn:	"Well ... no."
David:	"Having said that, then who controls your provocative behavior when you choose it?"
Marilynn:	"I don't like to admit it ... but I guess it all comes back to me. But, where the hell does that leave me? I'm a loser then, and I am making the choice."
David:	"You got it, but the important part is this. If you can choose provocative behavior, you can make a better choice. Or for that matter, you can make a worse choice, but either way who is it up to?"
Marilynn:	"Oh God, I'm worn out. If I had known this probation shit was going to be so hard, I would have run away. Isn't the time up yet?"

Marilynn has worked hard, and I don't want to do too much now. She has experienced a little success, and I want to build upon that. But any more right now might be too much.

David:	"Yeah, you are right, our time is up. Marilynn, I'm proud of you. You really worked hard today. We will look at some other things next time that might help you feel good without getting in trouble with the law. Will that be O.K.?"

Marilynn nodded, shook my hand and left.

Third Session

Marilynn:	"I have something to show you. Guess what it is?"
David:	"I'm not psychic Marilynn. Does it fall within the realm of lawful?"
Marilynn:	"Of course, I'm through with trying to seduce you. For now."

She produced a grade card and offered it to me for my review. She sat back in her chair and smiled broadly. I looked at the grade card. It was filled with Bs, one C and an A in social studies.

David: "That's great! Wow! You must be extremely proud!"

Marilynn's demure changed from happiness to sadness.

Marilynn: "I was, until you said I should be proud."
David: "What is the matter with feeling proud for excellent work?
              I would be delighted with these kinds of grades when I was
              your age."
Marilynn: "Oh shit. You don't know what you are talking about.
              I shouldn't have the A."
David: "Well, you have the A, so what's wrong with that?"
Marilynn: "I got it by flirting and letting old Henderson know that he
              could bang me if he wanted to. He wouldn't have given me an
              A if I had been straight."
David: "You don't know that, and besides, what's done is done. What
              are you going to do in the present six weeks?"
Marilyn: "What do you mean?"
David: "You and your brother have bicycles don't you?"
Marilynn: "Yes, why? You are always going off on these tangents, and I
              never know what you are going to ask me. What do bicycles
              have to do with old Henderson and social studies and my A?"
David: "Bear with me Marilynn, and you'll see. If you rode your
              bicycle to the store and realized you were riding on a very
              low tire, and if you continued it would probably ruin it, what
              would you do before you started home?"
Marilynn: "Oh God. I know the answer teach, FILL IT WITH AIR! Do I
              get an A?"

David: "Of course, you would fill it with air. If you rode it back the same way you rode it in what would it do?"

Marilynn: "It would ruin the tire. So you are saying I have to stop flirting with old Henderson, or my tire will be ruined? Is that it?"

David: "If you keep doing the things that brought you to this court, your tire on your bicycle won't be ruined, but your life bicycle tire may be ruined. How might your life bicycle tire be ruined?"

Marilynn: "I'll get sent to a girls' reformatory. Is that the message you are giving me with that stupid bicycle story?"

David: "Well, I try. You seem to get the idea though, is that correct?"

Marilynn: "Yes, yes, I get the idea. So what's next. What other great gems of wisdom are you going to give me?"

David: "Just a question, that's all. What are you going to do in Henderson's class this six weeks?"

Marilynn: "I'm going to behave like a good little virgin. Are you happy?"

David: "I'm not sure. What does behaving like a good little virgin look like?"

Marilynn: "I will keep my hands off him and quit propositioning him. Happy?"

David: "And if your grade goes down from an A, what will you do?"

Marilynn: "I will continue to behave even if he gives me an F. There. Now what?"

David: "To keep from getting a lower grade than an A and to keep from propositioning him, what can you do to keep that A?"

Marilynn: "God, you never quit. Study, study, study. Now can I get off probation?"

David: "Yes, you can get off probation but not right now. If you keep this contract and all the other rules the court set out in the adjudication and sentencing, then I will approach the judge and see about setting a date. O.K.?"

Marilynn continued on probation for six months, and there were no more referrals. Her grades continued to improve, and when I checked with Mr. Henderson, he said there was a distinct change that he saw in Marilynn in his class.

After probation, Marilynn kept in contact with me for several years. The last I heard from her, she had been married for a number of years and her dream of a little boy and a little girl had come true. The last thing she wrote was, "I'm making better choices now. Thanks."

Allen

The second scenario involves Larry and a probationer named Allen.

Allen, 16-years-old, was on probation for a number of violations. He had weekly individual appointments at the juvenile court from 4:00 p.m. to 4:50 p.m. On some occasions, he was seen with his parents.

When he would report for his probation session, the conversation went something like the following.

Larry:	"Hi, Allen. It's good to see you."
Allen:	"I need to leave. I have other things to do."
Larry:	"Allen, what do you have to do?"
Allen:	"I just don't want to be here."
Larry:	"You know I have set this time aside for you."
Allen:	"Can I leave?"
Larry:	"Tell me what you did this week?"
Allen:	"Nothing. Can I leave?"
Larry:	"Allen, the judge placed you on probation, and I have to see you on a regular basis in order to see how we can work together so that you don't have further violations. What can I do to help you?"
Allen:	"You can let me go now."
Larry:	"You can leave at 4:50. Tell me about school."

Allen:	"It's boring. Can I leave?"
Larry:	"Is it 4:50?"
Allen:	"No. Can I leave?"

As you can see, Allen only talked about leaving from the moment he arrived until he left. Larry, believing the behavior was manipulation, kept him until 4:50. Attempts to engage in meaningful conversation were unsuccessful. Attempts to play checker or chess were also unsuccessful. Sometimes, in frustration, Larry would tell Allen that talking about something was up to him. Allen could talk about anything that he wanted to talk about. Larry would be there for him but would be doing paperwork until he made the decision to talk. On a few occasions, Allen was allowed to leave at 4:45, but for most of the sessions during the next three months, he stayed until 4:50 p.m.

During the 12 weeks of seemingly nonproductive probation sessions, Allen's grades improved as did his behavior at home. Allen did not have any new contact with the police.

Allen's improvement in his grades and behavior at home cannot be explained by any insight gained through the probation sessions. It can be explained through the relationship developed between the probation officer and Allen. The officer, Larry, cared enough to keep Allen for the hour set-aside for his appointment, and Larry "never gave up."

After three months, Allen's appointments were reduced to every other week and then to once a month. His behavior at home, in school and in the community remained good. His grades improved to the A, B and C level. His case was successfully closed with no additional violations after nine months. This referral to juvenile court was his only one. Don't give up.

The Psychosomatic

Perhaps no scenario makes the point of not giving up any more than the following one involving Dr. William Glasser.

"To illustrate what a counselor can do, I would like to share with you the most dramatic incident I have ever been involved in as a psychiatrist. It occurred in 1956 while I was working as a resident on the psychosomatic ward of the Wadsworth Veterans Administration Hospital in West Los Angles. A forty-year old man who had been suffering from intractable asthma for the past ten years had been given every known medication with essentially no relief. His lungs were scarred and clogged as if his immune system had been attacking his bronchioles. He could hardly breathe; it was difficult for him to talk, and he had been put on a positive pressure respirator once or twice a week to keep him alive during the attacks he frequently suffered. The medical resident who called me in told me his condition was hopeless, but if I wanted to try to help him, I could see him.

"The man's human relations were nonexistent. He was in the dry-cleaning business with his brother, but he could do so little that they were not on good terms. This hospital admission has lasted six weeks, and the medical staff doubted they could ever get him in good-enough shape to leave the hospital. The man could barely talk, but I was patient and told him that even though it was hard, I was determined to counsel with him.

"I saw him for several weeks almost every day, and we gradually got acquainted. He kept telling me it was worthless; he needed good medical care, not a psychiatrist. But I persisted. Several times, he had a mild attack of not being able to breathe during the sessions and begged me with gestures to let him go back to the ward, but I told him that even if he couldn't talk, this was our time together and I didn't want him to go back until it was up.

"He seemed to be doing a little better, and I was encouraged. But then he got an attack so severe that I had to call the respirator crew, who put him on a respirator and wheeled him back to his bed. I got the idea that he was choosing the attack to get away from me and from having to talk about his present life. I decided that when he had the next attack, I would keep counseling even while he was on the respirator and he could respond with his hands or nod to my comments. The next attack was the worst yet. The respirator crew pumped and pumped but couldn't seem to get enough air into him, and he turned blue. The respirator crew, the medical resident, and, of course, the patient thought I was crazy. I paid no attention; I continued to counsel and could see his expression get more and more desperate.

"This went on for about twenty minutes, when suddenly he ripped the respirator from his mouth and nose and screamed at me, "For Christ's sake, I'm dying. Won't you leave me the f**k alone?"

"I said, 'No, I won't leave you alone. You need counseling and I'm not going to give up. You seem OK now; let's go on.

"And he was OK. His face, which had been blue-black from anoxia, had a little color, and he seemed to be breathing easier after the outburst than I had ever seen him breathe. We continued, and his breathing took a sharp turn for the better.

"The man stayed in the hospital for another two weeks getting his strength back but then was discharged. His lungs were badly scarred and he had to walk slowly, but he was able to breathe well enough to take care of himself. He came back to see me as an outpatient three or four times and said he thought he could handle things on his own.

"The key in this therapy was his trying to push me away and my not letting him do it. When I persisted, it was as if something had happened that he had never dreamed would. As much as he tried, he could not get me to reject him. It was enough to help him get back into some kind of control. His lungs were damaged, but he could breathe and take care of himself. There is tremendous power in good counseling. The medical resident who witnessed that dramatic episode was astonished and, truthfully, so was I. What I learned was never to give up, and I don't."

(Glasser, *Choice Theory*)

Summary

Giving juveniles praise, approval, rewards and touch is an important part of maintaining relationships with the youth. Because juveniles have had a lifetime of inappropriate and irresponsible behavior, you cannot expect them to change overnight. Your role is to be an agent of change. Never give up.

Questions

1. Define the acronym P-A-R-T.

   _____

   _____

   _____

   _____

2. True/False. When juveniles try to push you away, you should not give up.

3 True/False. Having a juvenile look into your eyes is a gentle way of helping him or her stop crying.

4. Allowing juveniles to express their _____ and ask _____ is a part of the connecting process.

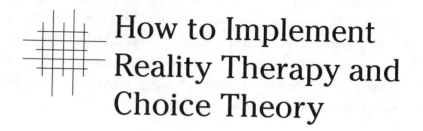

CHAPTER 12

How to Implement Reality Therapy and Choice Theory

Objectives

After reading this chapter, you will be able to:

- List four ways to implement Reality Therapy and Choice Theory within a juvenile facility
- Describe two examples of external control and internal control programs
- List 17 traits of effective treatment and interventions for juvenile offenders
- Identify the most difficult concept for staff in a correctional facility to comprehend and accept
- Describe the difference between Boss Management and Lead Management
- List six criteria for a quality school

Introduction

In this chapter, we will discuss how neither punishment nor external control programs (such as increased surveillance, home confinement, frequent drug testing, wilderness/survival programs, electronic monitoring, and boot camps) by themselves are effective at reducing recidivism. We will discuss what research studies say are effective treatment and intervention programs, and identify their common traits. We will discuss the four ways that Reality Therapy and Choice Theory can be successfully implemented in a facility: from the top down, within the education system, within a living unit, and within your own work and personal relationships. A major part of learning Reality Therapy and Choice Theory, in building better relationships, is giving up the seven deadly habits to control behavior-criticizing, blaming, complaining, threatening, punishing, nagging and rewarding to control.

How To Implement Reality Therapy And Choice Theory

Choice Theory says that the most significant problems we struggle with are caused by unsatisfying relationships. If this belief is true, then if we, as careworkers, do not improve our relationships with juveniles, we will have little success in helping them solve their problems. As careworkers, we see juveniles who engage in self-destructive behaviors. We see juveniles who do not have good parent-child and/or teacher-student relationships. We see juveniles who have acquaintances but not friends. To help juveniles make better choices, we need to help them improve their relationships with others—and that begins with us.

We believe that the best approach to implementing Reality Therapy and Choice Theory within a facility is from the top down. The tools have more influence if the entire facility adopts them as the foundation of the "treatment program." However, Reality Therapy and Choice Theory can be used one-on-one with youth or with groups of youth. The tools will be useful to you in your work with youth—even if your facility does not implement them in total, or from the top down.

From research studies and program evaluations, we have considerable knowledge about what works and what does not work. For example, a number of studies have found that punishment is not effective either as a deterrent or in reducing recidivism in the long run. Researcher Paul Gendreau's review of the literature concluded that various types of punishment—including regular incarceration and "scared straight" programs—actually produced higher recidivism rates than no punishment.

In *Preventing Crime: What Works, What Doesn't, What's Promising?*, Lawrence Sherman and several fellow researchers identified programs that by themselves were ineffective at reducing recidivism. These programs include: increased surveillance, psychodynamic or unstructured counseling, home confinement, regular probation services, frequent drug testing, wilderness/survival programs, electronic monitoring, and boot camps using traditional military basic training.

For the most part, these programs rely upon external control (monitoring) programs. Therefore, they lack the Reality Therapy component of obtaining a closer relationship with youths or clients.

Richard E. Redding, J.D., Ph.D., in *Characteristics of Effective Treatments and Interventions for Juvenile Offenders*, says that effective treatment and intervention programs share the following common traits.

- "They target medium- to high-risk juvenile populations.
- They target criminogenic risk factors, e.g., association with delinquent peers, school truancy, and substance abuse that are amenable to intervention.
- They are individualized, family-based, and delivered in community settings.
- They have well-trained staff, and a program director who is an effective advocate for the program with courts, parents, and community leaders.
- They deliver a sufficient treatment dosage (usually of at least six months duration).
- They have fidelity to the program design—the program must be delivered as designed, which requires well-trained staff, good supervision, and program monitoring and evaluation.
- The juvenile's treatment progress is monitored on an ongoing basis, with program modifications made as necessary.

- There is ongoing collaboration between the probation officer and treatment providers.
- Aftercare services are provided to prevent recidivism."

Redding goes on to identify certain treatments that show particular promise:

- "There is no single 'magic bullet' for rehabilitating juvenile offenders. A *combination of interventions*, tailored to the juvenile's individual needs, is generally required. "Service provision should be reconceptualized as an ongoing care model that emphasizes intervention in multiple spheres of an adolescent's life. The most promise lies in a comprehensive, long-term commitment, not in the development of any singular more powerful approach." (Tate et al., 1995)
- Programs showing the best hope of success are "individualized, community-based, family-oriented and multi-systemic, and include cognitive-behavioral interventions" (Tate et al. 1995)
- *Cognitive-behavioral approaches*, emphasizing social skills training and/or problem-solving skills training, appear to be among the most effective interventions. These approaches are designed to address juvenile offenders' poor social problem-solving skills and dysfunctional attributional processes in social situations, both of which have been linked to aggression.
- *Social skills training* may include, for example, anger management training and/or interpersonal or pro-social skills training.
- *Problem-solving training* may include, for example, the teaching of strategies for increasing self-control and social responsivity.
- *Behavioral programs and behavioral contracting* appear to be among the most effective interventions.
- *Parent management training* appears to be one of the most effective interventions for young offenders and for young children (under ages 12-13) showing aggressive or disobedient behaviors. It teaches parents effective discipline practices by manipulating reward contingencies to make positive behaviors more rewarding than negative behaviors.

- *Multiple service programs* that provide a range of treatment and intervention services (e.g., family therapy, intensive probation and case management, after-school programs, substance abuse treatment) appear to be among the most effective interventions."

We can tell by the research Redding is reviewing that the treatment programs evaluated were located both inside and outside juvenile facilities. Your facility may or may not be in community settings and/or where parents can easily be involved in the program. But regardless of where your facility is, we hope that you have:

- well-trained staff
- a program based on a particular treatment model or approach
- the ability to deliver a sufficient treatment dosage (usually of at least six months duration)
- a program that is delivered as designed which requires well-trained staff, good supervision, and program monitoring and evaluation
- a program that provides aftercare services to prevent recidivism.

We believe that Reality Therapy and Choice Theory fit the traits of successful programs and should be implemented from the top down in juvenile facilities. The following is an actual account of the early stages of implementing Reality Therapy and Choice Theory in a juvenile facility. We will follow David and his wife Sharon as they implement the treatment program in the Plainfield Youth Correctional Facility in Plainfield, Indiana.

Plainfield is located 15 miles west of Indianapolis, Indiana. The facility has 13 cottages for adjudicated delinquents. These youth range from 13 to 21 years of age, with a population in excess of 300 students. It is campus style and surrounded with a 15-foot fence, the top of which consists of razor wire.

In the spring of 2000, I (David) submitted a proposal for Reality Therapy training for the facility. The Council of Juvenile Correctional Administrators and the Indiana Department of Corrections approved a grant to cover the proposal.

On March 5, 2001, I (David) attended a morning planning meeting with Jane Burns, the Superintendent of the Plainfield facility, and six of her administrative staff: the Clinical Director, two Assistant Superintendents (one is Acting Principal of the onsite school for the students), the Clinical Social Worker, the Director of Security, and the Director of Training. The team decided that the initial training program would include 64 staff members. Staff would take both the Basic Intensive Week and the Basic Intensive Practicum courses. The Basic Intensive Week, a four-day course, would give staff a basic working knowledge of Choice Theory, Reality Therapy, and Lead Management.

The Basic Intensive Practicum is 30 to 32 hours of supervision in using Reality Therapy and Choice Theory and is scheduled for one full day for four months. It begins the first month after the Basic Intensive Week. The Basic Intensive Practicum gives staff the opportunity to practice the skills and knowledge they received during the Basic Intensive Week training. In short, the Practicum gives staff intensive training on how to implement Reality Therapy and Choice Theory in a facility for juveniles.

The Plainfield administrative staff, including the Superintendent agreed to, and each have, participated in a Basic Intensive Week.

Later that morning, I met with line staff, counselors and officers from several of the cottages to provide information and answer questions related to the forthcoming training. I asked if they would like to see things get better. They unanimously said, "Yes."

In the afternoon, I met with 12 students from the cottages. I explained to the students that Sharon and I travel throughout the United States. We work with staff and youth trying to help make things better, and now we have come to their facility. We asked if they would like for things to be better. The answer was a resounding "Yes," in a way that only kids can relay it.

Prior to the first Basic Intensive Week, 64 copies each of *Choice Theory* and *Reality Therapy in Action* were shipped to the facility. We asked the trainees to read these books prior to participating in the training. In addition, we gave the school faculty copies of *Every Child Can Succeed*, written by William Glasser in October 2000. Each of the 13 cottages received The Basic Concepts Poster. Trainees were encouraged to share information with the students in their cottages as well as other staff not scheduled for training.

As the training progressed, we began to find that some staff were sharing the *Choice Theory* book with the youth who wanted to read it. I (David) met with some of the youth. To my chagrin, I discovered that they had a better understanding of parts of Choice Theory than I had upon the completion of my Basic Intensive Week!

We conducted the initial course in April, June, August, and September. The Basic Intensive Practicum started in June 2001. As part of this course, we demonstrated relationship building with the students. We went into the cottages and worked with staff on getting involvement, teaching about choices, identifying total behavior and so forth.

The last cottage we visited consisted of the most difficult offenders—i.e., those who committed sex offenses, murders, assaults, and robbery. We spent three hours for four consecutive days working with the group of 32 youth who lived in the cottage. We spent the greatest part of the first day self-disclosing, making friends and asking for their help in making things better for themselves and the staff. The more we established our relationships, the more we found the youth to be less difficult to relate to and interact with than we had been forewarned.

Therefore, progress occurred as we worked hard at relationship building and as we used no external control. Involvement was a key element. Youth agreed to include reducing the amount of criticizing, blaming and complaining that they do in their behavior management plans.

A striking moment occurred when one of the youth said, "Staff shouldn't judge us on what we done before we got here. They made mistakes in their life too. They judge us and think we ain't as good as them, 'cause of stuff we done before we got here. They should judge us as we are right now."

I asked the youth, "Shawn, how could you reframe that so it isn't criticizing, blaming, complaining?" He hardly took time to think.

"I hope you staff will look at us today and help us as we try to do the right things."

WOW! There were several mouths gaping open as we saw this young man grasp the ideas and demonstrate the kinds of choices of which these youth are capable.

The approach to "build relationships" is the most difficult for some of the staff in a juvenile facility to comprehend and accept. Many Plainfield staff members verbalized the fear of losing power. Some staff believed that youth would take over the facility because they would be given too much power. These staff believed that youth should earn what they receive. Other staff quickly internalized the ideas of Choice Theory. These staff pointed out the power needs being displayed by their colleagues and urged them to "give it a try."

We have seen growth in many staff from the Basic Week to the Practicum. When I asked one skeptic if he tried these ideas and they didn't work, would he be any worse off? he grinned, and said, You are using that stuff, aren't you?" Then, he agreed to make a plan to implement some of the ideas in his cottage.

One staff member told Sharon that she wasn't going to use it because she used the Alcoholics Anonymous 12 Step program and believed in it. She stated that she saw many similarities in the 12 Step program with Reality Therapy and Choice Theory. She provided some examples.

Sharon asked the staff member if she would be willing to identify those parts with the Choice Theory terms to promote consistency through the facility. For example, the staff member might say to a youth: "When we do this part of Step X, your counselor would call that your quality world." She found that to be totally agreeable, and then she made a plan.

An unexpected boost to the program occurred in October of 2001. The state of Indiana mandated (boss management) that each juvenile facility use the Case Management system. This Case Management system outlines several policies that are to be implemented. One benefit to Reality Therapy training was evident in the document. Each facility is to "incorporate an effective treatment model that is a cognitive behavioral approach." Plainfield already had decided that Reality Therapy—a program that fosters change in thinking and, therefore, changes in behavior—would be the treatment model used in the facility.

The first training cycle concluded with our last visit in January 2002. For Sharon and I, the training was an exciting adventure, and we looked forward to each month's visit. We continued *our learning* with each visit to the facility.

With our help, the administration has begun to develop a training book that provides information on Reality Therapy and Choice Theory, the models for the facility's treatment program. This booklet will be used with new staff during orientation, and veteran staff during in-service training. At the end of this fiscal year, July 1, 2002, the facility will reevaluate their progress. They will schedule additional onsite visits by Sharon and me to help the implementation process continue.

The following page contains a letter from the superintendent.

STATE of INDIANA

DEPARTMENT OF CORRECTION

An Equal Opportunity Employer

PLAINFIELD JUVENILE CORRECTIONAL FACILITY
501 West Main Street
Plainfield, Indiana 46168-1297

February 12, 2002

TO WHOM IT MAY CONCERN:

As Superintendent of the Plainfield Juvenile Correctional Facility, I would like to make a few personal comments regarding the outstanding experience the staff and student population have gained through our interaction with our Choice Theory/Reality Therapy Consultants, David and Sharon Jackson.

This facility first became aware of the Jacksons in early 2001 when the institution was awarded a grant through the Council of Juvenile Correction Administrators. Research has shown Choice Theory/Reality Therapy can, and does, make a significant positive impact on the environment when properly trained and implemented, something the Plainfield Juvenile Correctional Facility felt we would like to further incorporate. Fortunately, this facility was placed in contact with David and Sharon Jackson, professional Choice Theory/Reality Theory Consultants. We have found David and Sharon Jackson to be quite knowledgeable of their subject matter, dedicated while being both very friendly and professional. They are masters at creating a non-threatening, accepting, learning environment, and inviting participation with the trainees, whether it be with our students or our staff.

The entire training process required the Jacksons to become closely involved with this facility for almost an entire year. Facility staff had the opportunity to blend together through the direction of the Jacksons; teachers, custody staff, counselors, behavioral clinicians, psychologists, recreation, health care and administration have all reaped remarkable benefits. The result has been an overall "better connected" staff. We attribute this phenomenon to the Choice Theory/Reality Theory Therapy training experience as presented by David and Sharon Jackson.

In summary, this facility has gained much from the training expertise as presented by David and Sharon Jackson. I certainly would not hesitate to recommend them for any future training endeavors that might arise. Please feel free to contact me directly for further information as needed.

Sincerely,

Jane Burns, Superintendent
Plainfield Juvenile Correctional Facility

JB/jy
Cc: file

230

Boss Management

There is another reason for Choice Theory being the foundation of the treatment program in a facility. Choice Theory helps reduce two relationship problems:

1) between careworkers and their supervisor
2) between teachers and students

Before we discuss boss management, we want you to generate some personal data that will help us explain the concept. Look at the 14 words listed below. Think back over the past six months or so and identify an incident that happened at work which you really felt good about. Once you have that event clearly in your mind, connect it with one or two of the following words. Then, put a "+" (plus sign) beside the word(s) you have chosen.

• Achievement	• Supervision
• Recognition	• Relationship with supervisor
• Work itself	• Work conduct
• Responsibility	• Salary
• Advancement	• Relationship with subordinates
• Growth	• Status
• Policy/Administration	• Security

What words are related to the positive event? Achievement? Recognition? Salary? Security?

Now think back over the same six months or so and think of an event that you thought that work was a real bummer—a time that you really felt bad about work. Connect the event with one or more of the 14 words. Then, put a "-" (minus sign) by the word(s) you have selected.

What words related to the negative event? Now draw a horizontal line across the list and between the words Growth and Policy/Administration.

For most people, positive events will be connected to the words listed above your line, above Policy/Administration. These words are Achievement, Recognition, Work Itself, Responsibility, Advancement, and Growth.

These things are free to the organization and tend to be free of external control. For example, an organization does not incur any cost when a supervisor says, "You really did a great job in talking with James. I was really impressed." Giving someone recognition or responsibility or a chance for personal or professional growth costs nothing.

Achievement, Recognition, Work itself, Responsibility, Advancement, and Growth are the things that give us satisfaction (meet our needs) at the workplace. These items are job satisfiers.

For most people, negative events will be connected to Policy/Administration, and the words listed after: Supervision, Relationship with Supervisor, Work Conduct, Salary, Relationship with Subordinates, Status, and Security.

These things are called job dissatisfiers and do not meet our needs. These items relate to our relationship with our supervisors, with management, with others in the organization, and with the organization itself.

Salary usually does not end up being associated with either the negative or positive event. For most of us, we do not get job satisfaction or job dissatisfaction from money.

We do not know the words you connected to either the positive or negative event. But having done this exercise hundreds of times with thousands of people, we believe that your personal data will fit into this pattern. Boss management is usually connected to job dissatisfiers and the use of fear and external control. Lead management is usually connected to job satisfiers and the use of personal involvement and internal control.

Many of us have had at least one boss, manager, or supervisor whose management style was just a little left of Attila the Hun. Or, we have at least read newspaper articles about a disgruntled employee taking a gun and killing several of their coworkers and/or supervisors. Being treated well at work is something that we all want—it is in our quality world, which we talked about in Chapter 5.

The following chart will point out some of the differences between Boss Management and Lead Management.

Boss Management	Lead Management
1) At all levels, the boss sets the task and the standards for how well the work is to be done and rarely consults workers about the quality or cost of the work.	1) Lead managers engage all workers in an ongoing, honest discussion of both the quality and cost necessary for the organization to be successful.
2) The boss usually tells, raher than shows workers how the job is done.	2) The lead manager, or someone designated by him or her, models the job so that the workers can see exactly what the manager expects.
3) The boss, or someone the boss designates, inspects the work.	3) The workers are responsible for inspecting their own work with the understanding that they know best what high quality work is and how to produce it at the lowest possible cost.

4) When the workers resist, the boss uses threats and punishment to try to make the workers do what he or she wants them to do.

4) The lead manager uses every chance he or she has to teach that the essence of quality is coninual improvement.

Reality Therapy and Choice Theory rely upon lead management. Therefore, implementing Reality Therapy and Choice Theory within a facility from the top down changes the management style and improves the relationships and productivity of all staff. *People support what they help build.*

We all know about "yell at the dog" theory. The husband and wife have a fight, and the one spouse yells at the dog as he or she walks out of the house. Unfortunately, "yell at the dog" is alive in some juvenile facilities—except that the juveniles are the low persons on the totem pole and the ones that get the verbal lashing. Implementing Reality Therapy and Choice Theory reduces, if not eliminates, this problem and enhances the relationship between the staff and the juveniles.

Quality Schools

In our work in probation, we realized that our probationers had to experience success in the home, in the community—and in school or work if they were not in school. At first, we believed that success at home was most important. As we worked with more juveniles, however, we learned that if they did not experience some success at school that their chances of successfully completing probation was nil.

Most of the juveniles in your facility are having problems with school and with the education system. They are turned off by **schooling** (making students acquire knowledge or memorize facts that have no value in the real world; forcing students to acquire knowledge that may have value in the real world but nowhere near enough value to try to force every student to learn it). Forcing people to learn has never been very successful. Therefore, we need to replace schooling with education—not acquiring knowledge but using knowledge—using what we have learned.

If Reality Therapy and Choice Theory are not implemented from the top down in your facility, they can still have a major influence on youth. Reality Therapy and Choice Theory can be implemented within the education system. In his books *The Quality School and The Quality School Teacher*, Glasser explains how Choice Theory can be used in schools. We refer you to both these books for a detailed description, which is beyond the scope of this workbook.

In brief, useful learning involves learning to speak, listen, read, and write, and to use these skills to solve problems. Quality schools do not try to force or use coercion on students to make them learn. Coercion only serves to remove schoolwork and teachers from the juveniles' quality worlds. To keep school-work in the students' quality worlds, teachers practice lead management and teach Choice Theory to both students and their families. The key to a quality school is good relationships.

Students in a quality school must do competent work, which is B level work in a traditional school. Students are urged to improve any of their good work until they and their teachers agree that it is now quality work—above the B level. Proficient students are offered jobs as teachers' assistants.

Glasser, in *Choice Theory*, says that there are, at a minimum, six criteria for a quality school:

1. "All disciplinary problems, not incidents, will be eliminated in two years. A significant drop should occur in year one.
2. "At the time the school becomes a quality school, achievement scores on state assessment tests should be improved over what was achieved in the past.
3. "TLC (total learning competency) means that all grades below compe-tence, or what is now a B will be eliminated. Students will have to demonstrate competence to their teachers or to designated teachers'

assistants to get credit for the grades or courses. All schooling will be eliminated and replaced by useful education.

4. "All students will do some quality work each year—that is, work that is significantly beyond competence. All such work will receive an A or higher grade. This criterion will give hardworking students a chance to show that they can excel.

5. "All staff and students will be taught to use Choice Theory in their lives and in their work in school. Parents will be encouraged to participate in study groups to become familiar with Choice Theory. A few of these groups will be led by teachers to start, but parent volunteers will be asked to take the groups over once they begin.

6. "It will be obvious by the end of the first year that this is a joyful school."

These Steps Apply to Anyone Working with Juveniles in or Out of a Juvenile Facility.

As a juvenile staff member—probation officer, counselor, juvenile careworker, teacher, kitchen worker, maintenance staff, custodian or any other position within or outside the facility—you can use Reality Therapy and Choice Theory to help youth build a better relationship with a meaningful adult.

You will encounter two different kinds of clients, students, juveniles, prisoners, patients, and so forth. (For purposes of this workbook, these terms mean the same thing.)

Voluntary clients are those juveniles who voluntarily work with you to get some help. These youth are willing to accept help based on the rules of the facility or organization for which you work. They are looking for solutions for a better way of living their lives. In short, they usually approach you about a problem they are having and seek your help.

Involuntary clients are those juveniles who are sent to you. They are generally not happy with the idea of relating with you. You are trying to persuade the youth to accept help within the boundaries of your organization's rules. Most delinquents fall into this category.

For both kinds of clients, a good relationship is essential but even more critical for the reluctant or involuntary client. Initially, establishing a relationship usually is more difficult with involuntary clients because they are expecting you to use external control psychology with them. After all, freedom of choice is the big difference between the voluntary and the involuntary client.

Voluntary clients can choose (or have chosen) whom they want to see or if they want to see anyone.

Involuntary clients have been told, ordered (external control) to see you or someone like you. Some careworkers say: "I'm not treatment or counseling staff, so my responsibility is to make sure that that the juveniles [clients] behave themselves and follow the rules of the facility." Juveniles naturally are more involuntary to careworkers than voluntary. Careworkers are responsible for the day-to-day, moment-to-moment supervision of the juveniles' activities in the facility. However, custody work not being part of treatment simply is not true.

Careworkers are constantly in the role of modeling behaviors. If careworkers establish good relationships and avoid the deadly habits (criticizing, blaming, complaining, threatening, punishing, nagging, and rewarding to control), juveniles will be more likely to learn better ways of behaving (prosocial skills).

The better the relationship careworkers have with juveniles, the more likely they will behave like voluntary clients. Conversely, the poorer the relationship careworkers have—meaning the more external control psychology is used—the more likely juveniles will continue behaving like involuntary clients.

The probation officer, although not normally in daily contact with delinquent youth, is still in a role of supervising youths' behavior. The probation officer certainly is in the position of teaching because all counseling or therapy is teaching. Like careworkers, probation officers can pursuade juveniles to move in the direction of voluntary clients by building a good relationship with them. Probation officers must be careful building relationships, however. Actions such as inviting juveniles home for dinner are inappropriate.

Let's listen in as David works with Joe, a juvenile who requested (a voluntary client) to see David about a problem.

Joe, a 16-year-old white male, was adjudicated delinquent after being arrested for selling ecstasy to elementary school children. He had $3,000.00 cash in his possession and admitted he got it from the young children for the drugs.

I have seen Joe a few times in the detention facility and have talked briefly with him. But I did not have any other contact with him until he requested to see me. Joe is a voluntary client, which is a bit unusual. Delinquents generally don't request to see a member of the staff about a problem. Juveniles usually have a complaint. This proved to be the case with Joe.

David:	"Hi Joe, come on into my office. It's good to see you."
Joe:	"You won't think so when I come in."
David:	"Wow! That sounds ominous. What do you have in mind for me?"
Joe:	"I didn't mean that as a threat. I just got some crap I'm not happy with in this dump, and you seemed like a guy who I could gripe to."
David:	"O.K., tell me what is on your mind."
Joe:	"Do you want it numerically or alphabetically?"
David:	"Well Joe, why don't you choose?"
Joe:	"O.K. first it's the g****n food. Then, there's the stupid staff."
David:	"How about the bed and rooms?"
Joe:	"Yeah, they suck too."
David:	"The temperature?"

Joe:	"You are a shithead too. You're just making fun of me."
David:	"I'm sorry Joe, but I'm just trying to speed this up. You are really using the deadly habits, and I just wondered if there is anything you can think about that is right or good about this place or the people in it?"
Joe:	"Deadly habits? What's that?"
David:	"They are criticizing, blaming, and complaining and other negative things. I just find it hard to get to know each other if we spend our time using those deadly habits, and I would like for us to become friends. Is that O.K.?"
Joe:	"I guess so, but why?"
David:	"Because I kind of like you. When I saw you in detention you always spoke to me, and we chatted a couple of times and it seemed O.K."
Joe:	"That's pretty weird wanting to be friends with any of us here in this place."
David:	"Well, I think it can be pretty hard to get to know someone unless you can talk about things, people, places and ideas that each person likes. Don't you think so?"

I have just begun to teach Joe a little Choice Theory. People, places, things and ideas that are important to us are perceptions, or pictures which each of us have in our quality worlds. Our quality world is that symbolic place in our heads for all the need satisfying pictures that we want. They are those things that feel good to us and satisfy our needs. Too often, delinquents have things in their quality worlds that are against the law. Our challenge is to help juveniles find lawful things to replace those negative pictures that continue to be the basis of the delinquent's unlawful thinking and acting.

| Joe: | "You are beginning to blow my mind. I don't think I know what the hell you are talking about." |

David: "Anything you don't understand, just ask me to explain it further. Hey, if you could do anything you wanted to do right now that is within the law, what would it be?"

Joe: "It wouldn't be staying in this dump, that's for sure."

David: "What you wouldn't do isn't very helpful. What would you like to be doing?"

Joe: "I'll play the game. I'd like to be on a Harley."

David: "I know very little about them, educate me."

Joe: "My uncle had an old dirt bike, he said it was an old H-D. But, he got a newer one and that is the one he let me ride on."

David: "What was it? A racing bike or what?"

Joe: "Naw. It was a dirt bike, and you rode it out in the pastures and in places where there weren't houses and stuff. It was fun."

David: "Did you ever crash?"

Joe: "Oh yeah. The first time he let me ride it by myself I tried to go between two trees, and there wasn't room. I really scratched my knuckles and really pissed my uncle. He wouldn't let me ride it for a long time after that."

David: "Man, they can be really dangerous can't they?"

Joe: "Yeah, but when he let me ride it again I was real careful, and he said he guessed I had learned me a lesson."

David: "Do you want one of your own someday?"

Joe: "Oh yeah, but I'd rather have a car."

David: "What kind?"

Joe: "I kind of like a Mercury."

David: "Sounds like you have a cool uncle, maybe he can help you figure out how to work and save your money to buy a car or a cycle."

Joe: "He is no more."

David: "What do you mean?"

Joe: "He was killed. He was robbin' a Quick Trip, and the clerk shot him in the head."

David:	"Wow. What do you think about that?"
Joe:	"I don't."
David:	"Did you go to his funeral?"
Joe:	"Nah. Funerals aren't cool."
David:	"Do you miss him?"
Joe:	"Nah. I miss his bike."
David:	"I had an uncle sort of like yours once, but he died too."
Joe:	"Did you go to his funeral?"
David:	"No, I was in the army overseas and couldn't get back. I cried though; I really liked him."

The youth was suddenly very quiet. We didn't talk for several seconds.

Joe:	"I cried too. But I got over it real quick."

This statement is a good sign. Joe isn't as void of feeling as he would have me think.

Joe:	"Are we going to talk about what I came in here to talk about?"
David:	"Sure Joe. You can talk about anything you choose to. What would you like to talk about?"
Joe:	"Don't you want to know why I asked to talk to you?"
David:	"Tell me why."
Joe:	"The staff are picking on me. They don't like me."
David:	"Explain to me what you mean when you say staff."
Joe:	"There's this one dude on the evening shift, and he is always making fun of how I walk."
David:	"So. It is just one staff member?"
Joe:	"Yeah. Mr. Fitzgerald. He doesn't like me."
David:	"What's one good thing that happens between you and Mr. Fitzgerald?"

He sat thinking for several seconds before he answered me.

Joe: "Sometimes, he smiles and asks me how my day has been but that doesn't happen often."

David: "Do you ever smile at him and ask him how his day has been?"

Joe: "Hell no! I'm a prisoner, and he is a guard. What's to smile about?"

David: "What's to smile about? Well, let me ask you this. If you thought that a smile and a question of how his day was, from you, would make things better would you be willing to try it?"

Joe: "Why should I be the one that does it first?"

David: "I don't know. Can you think of any reason to do it first?"

Joe: "No, why me? He makes me be grumpy most of the time."

David: "Come on Joe. Makes you grumpy? If you don't want to be grumpy can anyone make you be grumpy or do anything else if you don't want to?"

Joe: "I wouldn't be grumpy if he acted different toward me."

David: "Come on Joe, whose behavior can you control, and whose behavior can Mr. Fitzgerald control?"

Joe: "Mine, and his own, but if he was a friendlier guy, I would feel happier."

David: "What could you do when Mr. Fitzgerald comes on duty that would show him you are feeling good, or want to feel good?"

Joe: "I don't know. If I knew, I'd do it. Tell me what to do, and I'll do it."

David: "No you won't. You've already chosen to be a grump until Mr. Fitzgerald shows he is in a good mood."

Joe: "Look, if I said I'd do something different, I will. Are you calling me a liar?"

Reality Therapy and Choice Theory

David:	"Not at all. I just said you have already chosen to behave a certain way. If you wanted to behave a different way, what would you do?"

I refuse to revert back to external control psychology even though Joe is expecting it. Instead, I will continue to talk to Joe about his choices.

Joe:	"I don't know what I would do. Tell me the answer."
David:	"I don't know the answer. If I knew, I would tell you, but I have a suggestion if you are interested?"
Joe:	"Yeah, yeah, yeah, but I ain't brown nosing him. What's your suggestion?"
David:	"Well, before I give my suggestion, I guess I need to know what you mean when you say brown nosing."
Joe:	"That means stuff like telling him he is the greatest worker here and shit like that."
David:	"Would smiling at him when he comes on duty and asking him how his day has been come under the category of brown-nosing?"
Joe:	"I guess not."
David:	"You guess not?"
Joe:	"O.K. so no, is that your advice?"
David:	"I don't know. I'm just thinking. It would be something different for you to do, and even if it didn't work, would you be any worse off?"
Joe:	"I guess not."
David:	"You guess not?"

I'm pressing Joe again on his "I guess not" answer because I'm working toward persuading him to make a commitment to a plan of action.

Joe:	"No it wouldn't be any worse; there, you satisfied?"

David: "I'm not the one unhappy with Mr. Fitzgerald. What are you going to do?"

Joe: "I'll try it."

David: "What are you going to try, Joe. Explain it to me. You are having a great deal of difficulty with this idea, so tell me what you will try."

Joe: "I'll smile and ask him how the hell has his day been?"

David: "If you ask it like that, does that sound very friendly to you?"

Joe: "I'll smile and ask him how his day is. If he gives me any shit ..."

David: "Whoa, hold on a moment. Let's just stay with the positive stuff, O.K.? If you shoot at the basket and miss it the first time, do you quit shooting the basketball?"

Joe: "No, I keep trying."

David: "So? What are you going to do with Mr. Fitzgerald?"

Joe: (Grinning) "God, you never give up do you? So I'll ask friendly, can I go now?"

Even though our time is almost up, getting a stronger commitment from Joe on his plan is important.

David: "Let me ask you one more thing before we quit, O.K.?"

Joe: "Yeah, O.K. What is it?"

David: "I really think you have come up with a good plan, I'm proud of you Joe. When will you do this?"

Joe: (With a frown on his face) "I'll do it tonight when Mr. Fitzgerald comes on duty."

David: "And just what will you do and say to him? I'm very interested. Show me what you will do."

Joe: (Smiling) "I'll smile at him and I'll say, 'Hi Mr. Fitzgerald, how has your day been?' God, that's awful close to brown nosing."

David:	"What difference does it make if it makes it better for you? I'm serious, what difference does it make?"
Joe:	"Well, if it makes it better, I guess none."
David:	"Now, if it is all right with you, I would like to share with Mr. Fitzgerald what you are going to do so he won't think you are losing your mind." (I grinned as I asked this question.)
Joe:	"I guess so, O.K."
David:	"I'll be real curious how this works out. Will you tell me in the morning before breakfast? I'll leave word that you can stop by my office on your way to breakfast. O.K.?"

Joe seemed pleased with my interest.

Joe:	"O.K. See you in the morning."

The purpose of the last two questions and the request to stop by my office is to get as firm a commitment from Joe to the plan as I can and to build in accountability.

I talked with Mr. Fitzgerald, and even though he was skeptical, he agreed to give Joe the benefit of the doubt. Joe carried out his plan with Mr. Fitzgerald, and it worked out well. By the time the week was over, Mr. Fitzgerald also was smiling when he entered the facility each evening. Other careworkers commented on the new atmosphere between the two.

If, for some reason the plan had not worked, I would have not given up. I would have encouraged Joe to start another plan until he experienced success. Once a juvenile has a little success, we can then build upon that success.

Summary

Reality Therapy and Choice Theory can be implemented in a facility in a number of ways:

- From the top down, which we believe is the most effective and which has the most influence within the facility
- Within the education system
- Within a living unit or a cottage
- Within your own work and personal relationships

Implementing Reality Therapy and Choice Theory in a facility helps improve relationships and the productivity of the staff.

Questions

1. Increased surveillance, psychodynamic or unstructured counseling, home confinement, regular probation services, frequent drug testing, wilderness/survival programs, electronic monitoring, and boot camps. These programs are examples of _____ control programs.

2. Richard E. Redding, in *Characteristics of Effective Treatments and Interventions for Juvenile Offenders*, lists eight characteristics of effective treatment and intervention programs. Please list five.

   - _____

   - _____

   - _____

   - _____

   - _____

3. The approach to "_____ _____" is the most difficult for some of the staff in a correctional facility to comprehend and accept.

4. List the best approach to implementing Reality Therapy and Choice Theory within a facility.

_____

5. Job _____ include achievement, recognition, work itself, responsibility, advancement and growth.

6. Job _____ include policy/administration, supervision, relationship with supervisor, work conduct, salary, relationship with subordinates, status and security.

7. Most of the juveniles in your facility are having problems with school and are turned off by _____ (making students acquire knowledge or memorize facts that have no or little value in the real world).

8. List three traits of Lead Management.

- _____

- _____

- _____

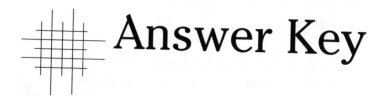 # Answer Key

CHAPTER 1

History and Overview

1. Four books written by Dr. William Glasser are: (choose four)
   - *Reality Therapy in Action*
   - *Counseling with Choice Theory: The New Reality Therapy*
   - *Reality Therapy: A New Approach to Psychiatry*
   - *Choice Theory: A New Psychology of Personal Freedom*
   - *Positive Addiction*
   - *The Identity Society*
   - *Control Theory*
   - *Control Theory in the Practice of Reality Therapy: Case Studies*
   - *Schools without Failure*
   - *Mental Health or Mental Illness?: Psychiatry for Practical Action*
   - *Unhappy Teenagers: A Way for Parents and Teachers to Reach Them*

2. Glasser's concern that the words **control theory** were adding to the misuse and misunderstanding of Reality Therapy lead to choice theory.

3. Both Control Theory and Choice Theory are examples of **internal** control psychology.

4. **False.** Choice Theory can benefit not only your work efforts but also your personal life.

5. Glasser believes that the problem of the world is **external control psychology.**

6. The three levels of external control are:
   - *An external stimulus makes us do something.*
   - *I can make you do something I want you to do even if you don't want to do it.*
   - *I will make you do it because it is right, even if I have to kill you to do it.*

CHAPTER 2

Basic Needs

1. The five basic needs that all of us have are the need to:
   - *Survive and reproduce*
   - *Belong and be loved*
   - *Have power*
   - *Have freedom*
   - *Have fun*

2. The physiological need is the need to survive and reproduce.

3. One of the hardest needs to meet in socially approved ways in a juvenile facility is the need for **power.**

4. David helped Josh and Jay T. satify their need for power by:
   - Asking for permission to pose questions
   - Asking for their ideas about improving their relationship

5. The need for **power** appears to be unique to our species.

6. Our need for power may cause direct conflict with our need to belong.

7. **Freedom** is so basic a need that people will give up their life fighting for it.

8. The day we stop playing is the day we stop **learning**.

9. **Needs** are our ultimate source of motivation.

10. **Needs** are **general** and universal.

11. **True.** Our needs are genetic.

12. **True.** Our behavior is how we choose to meet our needs.

CHAPTER 3

Choice Theory

1. The key parts of Choice Theory are:
   - *Basic needs*
   - *Your quality world*
   - *Total behavior*
   - *Your creative system*
   - *A new psychology of personal freedom*

2. Three things that can be eliminated as a topic of discussion in Choice Theory are: (choose three)
   - *Probing for the problem*
   - *Discussing the past*
   - *Complaining about people, places and things*

3. Personal freedom comes from giving up **external control** in our relationships with others.

4. The only **person** whose behavior we can control is our own.

5. The ten axioms of Choice Theory are:
   - *The only person whose behavior we can control is our own.*
   - *All we can give or get from other people is information. How we deal with that information is a choice.*
   - *All long-lasting psychological problems are relationship problems.*
   - *The problem relationship is always part of our present lives.*
   - *What happened in the past that was painful has a great deal to do with what we are today. But revisiting this painful past can contribute little or nothing to what we need to do now: improve an important, present relationship.*
   - *We are driven by five genetic needs: survival and reproduction, love and belonging, power, freedom, and fun.*
   - *We can satisfy our needs only by satisfying the pictures in our quality world.*
   - *All we can do from birth to death is behave.*
   - *All total behavior is designated by verbs, usually infinitives and gerunds, and named by the component that is most recognizable.*
   - *All total behavior is chosen, but we have arbitrary control over only the acting and thinking components. We can, however, control our feelings and physiology indirectly through how we choose to act and think.*

CHAPTER 4

Quality World

1. Three classifications of things we find in our quality world are:
   - *People we most want to be with*
   - *Things we most want to own or experience*
   - *Ideas or systems of belief that govern much of our behavior*

2. We choose to put people, things and ideas into our quality world that satisfy our basic needs.

3. We can fool our brains with **nonpeople** pleasure pictures (e.g., sex, drugs, alcohol) that produce feelings which are similar to how we feel when any need is satisfied.

4. Drugs can provide **pleasure**; they cannot provide **happiness**.

5. For happiness, we need **people** in our lives.

CHAPTER 5

Total Behavior

Exercises

Jerry

Acting

* *Watching the store*
* *Entering the store*
* *Looking at the unattended cash register, scurrying to it, and trying to force it open*
* *Walking away from the register and exiting the store*

Thinking

* *"If I steal the money, I'll go to prison."*
* *"I'm on probation, so I better do something different. Or, I'll make a bad choice and go to the slammer."*

Feeling

* *Upset, dismayed*
* *Anxious*
* *Relieved*

Physiology

* *Heart pounding*
* *Dry mouth*
* *Heart beating regularly*

<u>Answer Key</u>

Choice Theory Language

A. *Youth Worker:*   *"What do you think will happen if you continue choosing not to clean your room?"*

B. *Youth Worker:*   *"What are you going to do about this mess?"*

C. *Youth Worker:*   *"How are you going to handle this problem of being late?"*

D. *Youth Worker:*   *"It's movie night. Is what you're doing going to get you there?"*

1. All we can do from birth to death is **behave**.

2. The four components that make up our total behavior are:
   - *Acting*
   - *Thinking*
   - *Feeling*
   - *Physiology*

3. If what we are choosing to do is not satisfying the pictures in our quality world, we can:
   - *Change what we want*
   - *Change what we are doing*
   - *Change both*

4. Choice Theory uses the verb form because it is active and denotes control. Verbs put us in touch with the core philosophy of Choice Theory: We are choosing what we are doing, but we are capable of choosing something better.

5. The use of verbs in Choice Theory provides **hope** and **direction** to change.

6. Questions directed toward the acting and thinking components are most helpful in working with youth.

CHAPTER 6

The Creative System

1. Our creative system can influence **all** or **any** of the four components of total behavior.

2. Our creativity is **always** available, but we cannot **consciously** call it forth.

3. Connecting with youth means being friendly with and caring for them.

4. Once you have information about youths' interest, you should:
   - *Help them pursue those interests (acting)*
   - *Help them decide what and how to do it (thinking)*
   - *Ask how they feel about planning it (feelings)*
   - *Ask how their heart is working (physiology)*

CHAPTER 7

Introduction to Reality Therapy

1. According to William Glasser, having control means having control over our own lives and our choices.

2. An important part of Reality Therapy is **teaching** the steps to juveniles.

3. Good **relationships** are the key to healthy lives.

4. Responsibility is our ability to satisfy our needs without interfering with the ability of others to satisfy their needs.

5. You should talk to juveniles about their:
   - *Present life and relate it, when possible, to the juveniles' behavior*
   - *Interests, opinions, hopes, fears, and values (their ideas of right and wrong)*

6. **False.** If juveniles fail, you should not accept any excuses for their failure. You should help them see where they made the decision to do what they chose to do rather than do what was expected.

7. **False.** To focus on the present, you and the juvenile should search for the answer to "**What** is wrong?"

CHAPTER 8

Establishing a Working Relationship

1. The three steps of involvement that help you build a relationship with juveniles are:
   - *Be warm-friendly*
   - *Reveal yourself or self-disclose*
   - *Use pronouns I and me*

2. **Tolerance** is a fair and objective attitude toward those whose opinions, practices, race, religion, nationality, and so forth differ from your own. **Respect** is esteem for or a sense of the worth or excellence of a person. **Cooperation** is an act or instance of working or acting together for a common purpose or benefit.

3. Listening faults include: (choose five)
   - Deciding, even before the speaker starts, that the subject will be uninteresting and unimportant
   - Criticizing the speaker's delivery, clothes, haircut, or anything else

Reality Therapy and Choice Theory

- Becoming too involved in—and emotional—when questioning or opposing an idea
- Listening only for facts and skipping the details
- Trying to make an outline of everything
- Faking attention and withdrawing or daydreaming
- Tolerating or creating distractions
- Ignoring difficult material
- Over-reacting to certain words and phrases
- Mentally lining up arguments to counter what is said

4. Two questions that you should ask yourself to ensure that you are listening appropriately to juveniles are:
   - What is the juvenile telling me?
   - What does it mean to them?

5. Listening to the total message means listening to both the **verbal** and **nonverbal** parts of the message.

6. Four traits that you need to teach Reality Therapy are: (choose four)
   - *Being a responsible person*
   - *Being able to fulfill your own needs and being willing to discuss some of your own struggles*
   - *Possessing the strength to become involved, to withstand criticism or requests for sympathy, and to have your values tested by the juvenile*
   - *Investing a great deal of your time, energy and concern into the process*
   - *Showing that you care about what the juvenile does and believing that his or her values are important*
   - *Allowing the juvenile to go through emotional pain if it will help him or her learn about responsibility— "letting go"*
   - *Accepting the juvenile as he or she is*

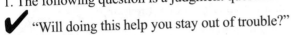

CHAPTER 9

Planning for Behavioral Change

1. The following question is a judgment question.

    ✔ "Will doing this help you stay out of trouble?"

2. Six traits of a good plan are: (choose six)
    - Simple
    - Attainable
    - Measurable, exact, precise
    - Short-range
    - Immediate
    - Controlled by the doer of the plan
    - Repetitive
    - Able to be revised
    - Personal
    - Positive
    - Evaluated
    - Process centered vs. outcome centered
    - Want and need fulfilling

3. The question you need to ask juveniles to move into the contract phase is: "What will you do next time?"

4. **False.** Once you make a contract with a juvenile, you must help the juvenile be successful by: giving reminders, discussing progress, and making a new contract.

5. **True.**

CHAPTER 10
Working with Groups

1. The acronym SAM stands for:
   - *Simple*
   - *Attainable*
   - *Measurable*

2. The purpose of the Chill Out Program is to expose youth to a number of moral dilemmas and help them learn to reason at a higher level.

3. **True.**

4. **True.**

5. Five social skills that juveniles need to learn and master are:
   - Beginning social skills (e.g., listening, asking a question, and saying thank you)
   - Advanced social skills (e.g., asking for help, joining in, and apologizing)
   - Skills for dealing with feelings (e.g., knowing your feelings and dealing with someone else's anger)
   - Empathy training (e.g., understanding the feelings of others)
   - Skills for dealing positively with aggression (e.g., negotiating, using self-control, and standing up for your rights without fighting)
   - Skills for defusing anger
   - Skills for dealing with stress (e.g., making a complaint, answering complaints, responding to failure, and dealing with an accusation)
   - Planning skills (e.g., deciding on something to do, making a decision, and concentrating on a task)

CHAPTER 11
Don't Give Up

1. The acronym P-A-R-T stands for:
   - Praise
   - Approval
   - Reward
   - Touch

2. **True.**

3. **True.**

4. Allowing juveniles to express their **opinions** and ask **questions** is a part of the connecting process.

CHAPTER 12
How to Implement Choice Theory and Reality Therapy

1. Increased surveillance, psychodynamic or unstructured counseling, home confinement, regular probation service, frequent drug testing, wilderness/survival programs, electronic monitoring, and boot camps. These programs are examples of **external** control programs.

2. Richard E. Redding, in *Characteristics of Effective Treatments and Interventions for Juvenile Offenders*, lists characteristics of effective treatment and intervention programs. These characteristics include: (choose five)
   - Target medium-to-high-risk juvenile populations
   - Target criminogenic risk factors
   - Are individualized, family-based, and delivered in community settings
   - Have well-trained staff

- Deliver a sufficient treatment dosage
- Have fidelity to the program design
- Monitor juvenile's treatment progress on an ongoing basis
- Have ongoing collaboration between the probation officer and treatment providers
- Provide aftercare services

3. The approach to **"building relationships"** is the most difficult for some of the staff in a correctional facility to comprehend and accept.

4. The best approach to implementing Reality Therapy and Choice Theory within a facility is from the top down.

5. Job **satisfiers** include achievement, recognition, work itself, responsibility, advancement and growth.

6. Job **dissatisfiers** include policy administration, supervision, relationship with supervisor, work conduct, salary, relationship with subordinates, status and security.

7. Most of the juveniles in your facility are having problems with school and are turned off by **schooling** (making students acquire knowledge or memorize facts that have no or little value in the real world).

8. Three traits of lead management are: (choose three)
- Engages all workers in an ongoing, honest discussion of both the quality and cost necessary for the organization to be successful.
- Models the job so that the workers can see exactly what the manager expects.
- Enables the workers to inspect their own work.
- Teaches that the essence of quality is continual improvement.

 # References

Glasser, Naomi, and Glasser, William, M.D., *Control Theory in the Practice of Reality Therapy— Case Studies*, New York, Harper and Row, 1989.

Glasser, William, M.D., *Reality Therapy*, New York, Harper and Row, 1965.

_____, *Schools without Failure*, New York, Harper and Row, 1969.

_____, *Choice Theory: A New Psychology of Personal Freedom*, New York, Harper-Collins Publishers, 1998.

_____, *Creating the Competence Based Classroom*, Chatsworth, California, The William Glasser Institute, 1999.

_____, *Every Student Can Succeed*, San Diego, California, Black Forrest Press, 2000.

_____, *Reality Therapy in Action*, New York, Harper-Collins Publishers, 2000.

_____, *Counseling with Choice Theory — The New Reality Therapy*, New York, Quill, 2001.

_____, *Fibromyalgia: Hope From a Completely New Prespective*, Chatsworth, California, William Glasser, Inc., 2001.

_____, *Unhappy Teenagers: A Way For Parents and Teachers to Reach Them*, New York, Harper-Collins Publishers, 2002.

Glasser, William, M.D. and Glasser, Carleen, M.Ed., *The Language of Choice Theory*, New York, Harper-Collins Publishers, 1999.

Wubbolding, Robert E., *Using Reality Therapy*, New York, Perennial Library, 1988.

_____, *Intensive Workshop Reality Therapy Training*, Center for Reality Therapy/Midwest, Cincinnati, Ohio, 1986.

Juvenile Offenders
with Mental Health Disorders
Who Are They? and What Do We Do With Them?
Lisa Melanie Boesky, Ph.D

This book is a practical, user-friendly guide for a variety of professionals who supervise, manage, teach, or treat juvenile offenders with mental health disorders. Although the content is primarily focused on juveniles in residential facilities (e.g., detention centers, training schools, diagnostic/reception centers, ranches, work camps, boot camps, group homes), the information is just as relevant and applicable to juvenile offenders on community supervision.

Dr. Boesky provides essential information to help professionals both *identify* and *manage* juvenile offenders with mental health disorders. (2002, 354 pages, 1-56991-154-1)

Chapters Include:

◆ Diagnosis of Juveniles with Mental Health Disorders
◆ Mood Disorders (Depression, Bipolar, Dysthymia)
◆ Attention-Deficit/Hyperactivity Disorder (ADHD)
◆ Oppositional Defiant Disorder and Conduct Disorder
◆ Posttraumatic Stress Disorder (PTSD)
◆ Schizophrenia and Other Psychotic Disorders
◆ Developmental Disorders (Mental Retardation, Learning Disabilities,
    Fetal Alcohol Syndrome)
◆ Treatment of Juveniles with Mental Health Disorders
◆ Suicide and Self-Injury/Self-Mutilation
◆ Co-Occurring Mental Health and Substance Abuse Disorders
◆ Female Offenders, Cultural Issues and Violence

"...an excellent and comprehensive resource for individuals entering the field of corrections – or for those who have been working in this field but who are frustrated in their efforts to respond in the most positive manner to juvenile offenders."

Nancy Cunningham, Psy.D.
Bureau Chief
Bureau of Correctional Health
Ohio Department of Youth Services

Call 1-800-222-5646, ext. 1860 to Order!
American Correctional Association
4380 Forbes Boulevard
Lanham, MD 20706-4322
www.aca.org

FOUNDED 1870